D0365351

Breakthrough Teaching and Learning

Tracy Gray · Heidi Silver-Pacuilla
Editors

Breakthrough Teaching and Learning

How Educational and Assistive
Technologies are Driving Innovation

 Springer

Editors
Tracy Gray, Ph.D.
American Institutes for Research
Washington, DC
USA
tgray@air.org

Heidi Silver-Pacuilla, Ph.D.
American Institutes for Research
Washington, DC
USA
hsilver-pacuilla@air.org

ISBN 978-1-4419-7767-0   e-ISBN 978-1-4419-7768-7
DOI 10.1007/978-1-4419-7768-7
Springer New York Dordrecht Heidelberg London

Library of Congress Control Number: 2011924545

© Springer Science+Business Media, LLC 2011
All rights reserved. This work may not be translated or copied in whole or in part without the written permission of the publisher (Springer Science+Business Media, LLC, 233 Spring Street, New York, NY 10013, USA), except for brief excerpts in connection with reviews or scholarly analysis. Use in connection with any form of information storage and retrieval, electronic adaptation, computer software, or by similar or dissimilar methodology now known or hereafter developed is forbidden.
The use in this publication of trade names, trademarks, service marks, and similar terms, even if they are not identified as such, is not to be taken as an expression of opinion as to whether or not they are subject to proprietary rights.

Printed on acid-free paper

Springer is part of Springer Science+Business Media (www.springer.com)

To our own insightful digital natives Jessica, Rachel, Gabriel, and Rosemary who have taught us so much about the wonders of technology.

Acknowledgments

We would like to recognize the authors who worked under very tight deadlines, with humor and a sense of mission to complete their chapters on time. In addition, we gratefully acknowledge the support from the American Institutes for Research (AIR, www.air.org) to work on this book. Specifically, we would like to thank our senior leadership, David Myers and Mark Kutner, for their encouragement to blend our lessons learned with the latest thinking about technology integration for teaching and learning. In addition, we would like to recognize Lara Bogle who was meticulous in her edits and suggestions. And finally, we give special thanks to our husbands, John Iwaniec and Nicholas Pacuilla for their understanding and support to complete this book, despite the hurdles that arose along the way.

Contents

Contributors

Turadg Aleahmad, Ph.D.
Candidate, Carnegie Mellon University, Pittsburgh, PA, USA
Turadq@cmu.edu

Elizabeth Bonsignore, Ph.D.
Candidate, University of Maryland, College Park, MD, USA
ebonsign@umd.ed

Alise Brann, Ed.S., M.S. Ed.
American Institutes for Research, Washington, DC, USA
ABrann@air.org

Chris Dede, Ed.D.
Harvard University, Cambridge, MA, USA
dedech@gse.harvard.edu

John Foley, Ph.D.
SUNY-Cortland, Cortland, NY, USA
John.Foley@cortland.edu

April Galyardt, Ph.D.
Candidate, Carnegie Mellon University, Pittsburgh, PA, USA
Agalyardt@gmail.com

Tracy Gray, Ph.D.
American Institutes for Research, Washington, DC, USA
tgray@air.org

Derek Hansen, Ph.D.
University of Maryland, College Park, MD, USA
Shakmatt@gmail.com

Steve Hargadon, B.A.
Elluminate/Blackboard Collaborate, Lincoln, CA, USA
Steve@hargadon.com

Scott Lapinski, M.Ed.
CAST, Wakefield, MA, USA
SLapinski@cast.org

Eric Morrison, M.A.
Pima Community College, Tucson, AZ, USA
Emorrison@pima.edu

Cynthia Overton, Ph.D.
American Institutes for Research, Washington, DC, USA
Coverton@air.org

Wei Qiu, Ph.D.
Webster University, St. Louis, MO, USA
Qiuwei1@msu.edu

Rebecca Reynolds, Ph.D.
Rutgers University, New Brunswick, NJ, USA
Rebecca.reynolds@gmail.com

David H. Rose, Ed.D.
CAST, Wakefield, MA, USA
DRose@cast.org

Michael Russell, Ph.D.
Boston College, Boston, MA, USA
russelmh@bc.edu

Heidi Silver-Pacuilla, Ph.D.
American Institutes for Research, Washington, DC, USA
hsilver-pacuilla@air.org

Stephen Yang, Ph.D., ABD
SUNY-Cortland, Cortland, NY, USA
stephen.yang@cortland.edu

Yong Zhao, Ph.D.
University of Oregon, Portland, OR, USA
yongzhao@uoregon.edu

Biography

Turadg Aleahmad, Ph.D. Candidate, Carnegie Mellon University
Turadg Aleahmad is a Ph.D. candidate in Human Computer Interaction at Carnegie Mellon University. He is also a fellow in CMU's IES-funded Program for Interdisciplinary Education Research and member of the NSF-funded Pittsburgh Science of Learning Center. Turadg's research focuses on adapting HCI design methods to the development of educational technologies that both inform and are informed by theories of learning. His dissertation applies these methods in creating a system to support students' time and attention management. Before CMU, he worked as a technologist at UC Berkeley developing the Web-based Inquiry Science Environment (WISE) and later the Scalable Architecture for Interactive Learning (SAIL).

Elizabeth Bonsignore, Ph.D. Candidate, University of Maryland
Elizabeth Bonsignore is a Ph.D. candidate in the iSchool at the University of Maryland, College Park. Her research interests are grounded in the study of New Literacies practices (Lankshear/Knobel) and Participatory Cultures (Jenkins), with a focus on the design of socially mediated, collaborative technologies to support them. Her methodological approaches stem from *Druin's* Cooperative Inquiry design philosophy, with a focus on school-aged children and young adults. Her initial design research involved the study of online communities for learning, such as Classroom 2.0. Current research with the University of Maryland's Human Computer Interaction Lab (HCIL) includes the design and use of collaborative storytelling technologies (StoryKit) and social learning sites for children, such as the National Park Service's WebRangers. To further develop and extend her New Literacies' scholarship, she is a research assistant for an NSF-funded project, Alternate Reality Games (ARGs) in the Service of Education and Design.

Alise Brann, Ed.S., M.S. Ed., American Institutes for Research
Alise Brann is a research analyst at American Institutes for Research, with expertise in the areas of special education, assistive technology, social media, and the use of digital tools in teaching and learning. Her work focuses on utilizing technology to facilitate access to academic content for struggling students, and students with learning and print disabilities on U.S. Department of Education projects such as the Center for Technology Implementation, The Center for Implementing Technology

in Education, The National Charter School Resource Center, and The National Center for Technology Innovation. Alise writes and blogs regularly for educators and parents on topics in educational technology, including info briefs and a monthly column on assistive technology solutions for LD Online, and runs the TechMatrix group on the assistivetech Ning. Alise received her Ed.S. in Assistive Technology, and M.S. Ed in Special Education from Simmons College and her B.A. in Psychology from Smith College.

Chris Dede, *Ed.D., Harvard University*
Chris Dede is the Timothy E. Wirth Professor in Learning Technologies at Harvard's Graduate School of Education. His fields of scholarship include emerging technologies, policy, and leadership. His funded research includes four grants from NSF and the U.S. Department of Education's Institute of Education Sciences to explore immersive simulations and transformed social interactions as means of student engagement, learning, and assessment. In 2007, he was honored by Harvard University as an outstanding teacher. Chris has served as a member of the National Academy of Sciences Committee on Foundations of Educational and Psychological Assessment and a member of the 2010 National Educational Technology Plan Technical Working Group. He serves on Advisory Boards and Commissions for PBS TeacherLine, the Partnership for twenty-first century skills, the Pittsburgh Science of Learning Center, and several federal research grants. His co-edited book, *Scaling Up Success: Lessons Learned from Technology-based Educational Improvement*, was published by Jossey-Bass in 2005. A second volume he edited, *Online Professional Development for Teachers: Emerging Models and Methods*, was published by the Harvard Education Press in 2006.

John Foley, *Ph.D., SUNY-Cortland*
John Foley, currently an associate professor of physical education at SUNY-Cortland, was recently elected to the position of president of the North American Federation of Adapted Physical Activity (NAFAPA). NAFAPA is an international organization dedicated to the conduct, implementation, and dissemination of research in the practice of adapted physical activity. John's work has focused on ways to increase the physical activity levels of individuals with disabilities and reduce the health disparity that exists between individuals with and without disabilities.

April Galyardt, *Ph.D. Candidate, Carnegie Mellon University*
April Galyardt is a Ph.D. candidate in Statistics at Carnegie Mellon University and a fellow of CMU's Program for Interdisciplinary Education Research. Her research is at the intersection of statistics, machine learning, and psychometrics. Current work uses statistical models to identify different strategies that students use during assessments. Prior to coming to CMU, April taught mathematics at Kishwaukee Community College, IL.

Tracy Gray, *Ph.D., American Institutes for Research*
Tracy Gray is a managing director at the American Institutes for Research where she directs two national technology centers funded by the U.S. Department of

Education, Office of Special Education Programs (OSEP) – the National Center for Technology Innovation (http://www.NationalTechCenter.org) and the Center for Technology Implementation. These Centers promote the development and implementation of evidence-based technology practices and tools to improve the educational achievement of students with disabilities. She also serves as the director for the Microsoft Math Partnership (http://www.mathpartnership.org) providing technical assistance to teachers, administrators, and coaches of mathematics to implement high-quality technology-enriched programs for middle-school students. Tracy is a recognized expert in education and technology who has led numerous initiatives in the nation and abroad that examine the impact of technology on educational achievement. Prior to joining AIR, she led the philanthropic initiatives to integrate technology in after-school programs as the vice president for Youth Services at the Morino Institute. She served as the first deputy executive director and chief operating officer for the Corporation for National Service that launched AmeriCorps. Earlier, Tracy served as the deputy director for the first American Red Cross AIDS Public Education program.

Derek Hansen, *Ph.D., University of Maryland*
Derek L. Hansen is an assistant professor at Maryland's iSchool and director for the Center for the Advanced Study of Communities and Information (http://www.casci. umd.edu), a multidisciplinary research center focused on harnessing the power of novel social technologies to support the needs of real and virtual communities. He is also an active member of the Human Computer Interaction Lab (http://www.cs. umd.edu/hcil/). Dr. Hansen received his Ph.D. from the University of Michigan's School of Information where he was an NSF-funded interdisciplinary STIET Fellow (http://www.stiet.si.umich.edu/) focused on understanding and designing effective online sociotechnical systems. His research focuses on the application and design of social media technologies, as well as methods for studying online communities.

Steve Hargadon, *B.A., Classroom 2.0*
Steve Haragdon is the social learning consultant for Elluminate/Blackboard Collaborate, founder of the Classroom 2.0 social network, host of the Future of Education interview series, and co-chair of the Global Education Conference. He pioneered the use of social networking in education, particularly for professional development. Steve blogs, speaks, and consults on educational technology, runs the Open Source Pavilion and speaker series for the ISTE, CUE, and other edtech shows, and is the organizer of the annual EduBloggerCon, OpenSourceCon, and the "unplugged" and "bloggers' cafe" areas at both ISTE and CUE. He is also the Emerging Technologies Chair for ISTE, the author of "Educational Networking: The Important Role Web 2.0 Will Play in Education," the recipient of the 2010 Technology in Learning Leadership Award (CUE), and a blogger at http://www. SteveHargadon.com. He has consulted for PBS, Intel, Ning, Microsoft, KnowledgeWorks Foundation, CoSN, the U.S. State Department, and others on educational technology and specifically on social networking. He and his wife have four children.

Scott Lapinski, *M.Ed., CAST*
Since joining CAST in 2010, Scott Lapinski has played a key role in the National UDL Center, where he writes and edits reports, literature reviews, and other Website content. Scott also supports the UDL Guidelines project, collecting, and analyzing qualitative and quantitative data on how the guidelines are used. He is helping to prepare version 2.0 of the Guidelines. Scott also contributes significantly to CAST's publications, and is a contributor to three current book projects as well as scholarly articles. Prior to joining CAST, Scott worked as an elementary school teacher in Massachusetts. Scott received his Bachelors degree in psychology from SUNY Stony Brook, and his masters in Elementary Education from Boston College.

Eric Morrison, *M.A., Pima Community College*
Eric Morrison has worked with the National Center on Technology Innovation (NCTI) since 2004. He has developed the *Innovator Profiles* from his research on the creation of technological systems for persons with disabilities. He uses Activity and Distributed Cognition Theories as primary lenses for understanding cognitive connections between humans and their technological agents in goal-directed activity. Eric serves as lead faculty at Pima Community College (PCC) in Tucson, Arizona, teaching Developmental Reading. He endeavors to increase both traditional and information literacy for students from diverse backgrounds, and is interested in the role of literacy in power relations and the promotion of equity. At PCC, Eric served as the head of disability support services for a decade, developing Assistive Technology and alternative media production infrastructure for multiple campuses and libraries. He also performed psycho-educational assessments to diagnose adult students with learning disabilities to qualify them for essential civil protections and services. Eric served the Association on Higher Education and Disability (AHEAD) as a two-term state chapter president in Arizona and has published on disability issues in various periodicals.

Cynthia Overton, *Ph.D., American Institutes for Research*
Cynthia Overton is a senior research analyst with American Institutes for Research (AIR) where she serves as the deputy director for the Center for Technology Implementation. While at AIR, Cynthia has served on various technology-related projects that aim to improve education outcomes for students with disabilities. She has delivered numerous presentations to inform the field on how technology can be used to enhance outcomes for individuals with disabilities both domestically and abroad. Cynthia holds M.S. and Ph.D. degrees in education with a concentration in educational technology from the University of Michigan and earned an Assistive Technology Applications Certificate from California State University, Northridge Center on Disabilities. She has conducted research on how college students with visual impairments use technology to engage with their learning environments and currently serves on the Advisory Board for Art Education for the Blind's Art Beyond Sight Museum Education Institute.

Wei Qiu, *Ph.D., Webster University*
Wei Qiu is an instructor designer at Webster University. She received her Ph.D. degree in educational psychology and educational technology from Michigan State

University. Her research focuses on social media, cultural adjustment, language learning, and distance learning.

Rebecca Reynolds, *Ph.D., Rutgers University*

Rebecca Reynolds is an assistant professor in the School of Communication and Information at Rutgers University. From 2009 to 2010, she was an AERA-AIR Post-Doctoral Fellow in Washington, DC, where she supported the work of the National Center on Technology Innovation (NCTI). She also conducts consultative evaluation and design-based research for the World Wide Workshop Foundation's Globaloria-West Virginia project. She holds a B.A. in Sociology from Tufts University, and an M.A. and Ph.D. from Syracuse University, where she studied in the Newhouse School of Public Communications, the School of Information Studies, and the School of Education. Prior to graduate school, Rebecca held key roles in product management and interactive marketing at Pearson's Family Education Network, ZDNet Ziff Davis, Peoplestreet, and TechTarget.

David H. Rose, *Ed.D., CAST*

David Rose, chief education officer at the *Center for Applied Special Technology (CAST)*, helped found the organization with a vision of expanding opportunities for all students, especially those with disabilities, through the innovative development and application of technology. David specializes in developmental neuropsychology and in the universal design of learning technologies. In addition to his role as founding director/chief scientist of cognition and learning at CAST, David lectures at Harvard University's Graduate School of Education, where he has been the faculty for 20 years. He has been the lead researcher on a number of U.S. Department of Education grants and now is the principal investigator for two national centers to develop and implement the National Instructional Materials Standard (NIMAS). He is the co-author of *Teaching Every Student in the Digital Age: Universal Design for Learning* (ASCD, 2002), as well as numerous other books and articles, and is frequently a keynote speaker at regional and national educational conferences.

Michael Russell, *Ph.D., Boston College*

Michael Russell is an associate professor in the Lynch School of Education and the director of the Nimble Innovation Lab at Measured Progress. Mike directs several projects, including the Diagnostic Algebra Assessment Project, the Student Accessibility Assessment System Project, the Accessible Mathematics Assessment Project, and a series of computer-based testing accommodation and validity studies. Mike is the founder and chief editor of the Journal of Technology, Learning, and Assessment. He has also been affiliated with the Center for the Study of Testing, Evaluation, and Educational Policy (CSTEEP) since 1994. His research interests lie at the intersection of technology, learning, and assessment and include applications of technology to testing and impacts of technology on students and their learning.

Heidi Silver-Pacuilla, *Ph.D., American Institutes for Research*

Heidi Silver-Pacuilla is a senior research analyst at the American Institutes for Research where she is extensively involved in several of AIR's technology projects. She has served as deputy director of the National Center for Technology Innovation

(NCTI) for the past 6 years as well as managed knowledge development and production of Web-based tools in the Teaching Excellence in Adult Education Center and Center for Implementing Technology in Education (CITEd). She provides training and technical assistance on a variety of projects addressing the needs of struggling students through innovative uses of technology and develops practitioner-friendly materials for a variety of print- and Web-based outlets. Heidi has published scholarly work in adult pedagogy, disability services, integration of technology into basic skills learning, service delivery systems, and women's literacy. She holds a Ph.D. from the University of Arizona in adult literacy and has served on the board of the National Coalition for Literacy for several years, including as the 2010–2011 president.

Stephen Yang, Ph.D. (ABD), SUNY-Cortland

Stephen P. Yang is an assistant professor at SUNY-Cortland and he researches the effectiveness of using exergames/active games and technologies for children, adolescents, and adults with and without disabilities. Yang has been active in the field of exergaming since its infancy and has published and presented internationally and nationally. Recently, he was invited to speak at the Game Developers Conference, Journal of Health Promotion Conference, NCTI Technology Innovators Conference, Indiana University, American Heart Association/Nintendo Summit (*The Power of Play: Innovations in Getting Active*) and two events in Seoul, South Korea for the Korean Serious Games Festival and Continua Alliance Fall Meeting. He works with the Games for Health (GFH) Project (http://www.gamesforhealth.org), consults with video game developers, and toy and exergame companies on products and programming. In recognition of his knowledge and expertise, he was appointed to the Board of Advisors of *Exergame Fitness* and he is a founding member of the *ExerGame Network (TEN)*. Throughout all his research and collaborations, Stephen wishes to see how exergames can be used as a potential gateway to inspire people of all ages and abilities to be active and healthy for a lifetime (http://www.exergamelab.blogspot.com).

Yong Zhao, Ph.D., University of Oregon

Yong Zhao is currently Presidential Chair and Associate Dean for Global Education, College of Education at the University of Oregon, where he also serves as the director of the Center for Advanced Technology in Education (CATE). He is a fellow of the International Academy for Education. His research interests include educational policy, computer gaming and education, diffusion of innovations, teacher adoption of technology, computer-assisted language learning, and globalization and education. Yong has extensive international experiences. He has consulted with government and educational agencies and spoken on educational issues in many countries on six continents. His current work focuses on designing twenty-first century schools in the context of globalization and the digital revolution.

Reshaping the Role of Technology in Education

Chris Dede

As this volume on *Breakthrough Teaching and Learning* describes, we live at a time when advances in information and communications technology (ICT)[1] offer incredible promise for improving learning and teaching. In particular, over the past few years, three developments have combined to reshape the role of ICT in education.

First, *Web 2.0 interactive media* are easy to access and use, free, and designed to support collaborative knowledge creation and sharing. An increasing number of users are progressing from media for sharing (social bookmarking and networking, photo and video sharing) to tools for thinking together (blogs and online discussions) to communities collaborating to accomplish shared goals (wikis and mashups). An increasing proportion of people in all age groups are using social media as the dominant means of informal learning, developing strengths and preferences in how they create and share knowledge and in what types of authority they accept as certifying its accuracy. As a growing number of students enter schools and colleges with beliefs and preferences about learning and knowledge based on social media, this will place disruptive pressures on these institutions to acknowledge types of learning and knowing discrepant with classic models of instruction, authority, and epistemology (Dede, 2008).

Second, *immersive interfaces* are enabling the design of rich virtual experiences accessible by learners even in contexts isolated from the real-world, like classrooms. Emerging multiuser virtual environment (MUVE) interfaces offer students an engaging Alice-in-Wonderland experience in which their digital emissaries in a graphical virtual context actively engage in experiences with the avatars of other participants and with computerized agents. As a complement, augmented reality

---

[1] ICT is a common acronym for information and communications technologies that is used widely internationally. Throughout this book, we have chosen to use the term "educational and assistive technologies" to draw attention to the role of technology in education and the critical need to ensure access for all learners, particularly those with disabilities.

C. Dede (✉)
Harvard University, Cambridge, MA, USA
e-mail: dedech@gse.harvard.edu

T. Gray and H. Silver-Pacuilla (eds.), *Breakthrough Teaching and Learning:
How Educational and Assistive Technologies are Driving Innovation*,
DOI 10.1007/978-1-4419-7768-7_1, © Springer Science+Business Media, LLC 2011

(AR) interfaces enable "ubiquitous computing" models. Students carrying mobile wireless devices through real-world contexts engage with virtual information superimposed on physical landscapes (such as a tree describing its botanical characteristics or an historic photograph offering a contrast with the present scene). This type of mediated immersion infuses digital resources throughout the real-world, augmenting students' experiences and interactions. Both these kinds of immersive interfaces enable "situated" learning in a detailed, simulated setting with embedded tacit clues, context-sensitive support, and salient features highlighted (Dede, 2009).

Third, the emerging infrastructure of powerful *mobile wireless devices* is complementing the classic infrastructure of workstations, laptops, and wires (Bjerede, Atkins, & Dede, 2010). Mobile wireless devices and associated ubiquitous apps have the potential to transform teaching and learning in K-20 schooling. When this potential is realized, students will benefit from 24/7 access to digital curriculum that is highly personalized with respect to level, pace, and learning style. Teachers will benefit from digital participation in communities of practice with global reach and from dashboards that actively display real-time data regarding their students' progress. As wireless education technologies allow learning to expand beyond the four walls of the classroom and the hours of the school day, teachers will gain flexibility in how they can use precious classroom minutes.

The U.S. 2010 National Educational Technology Plan (NETP) provides an overview of these and other recent developments with promise to transform teaching and learning (U.S. Department of Education, 2010). The NETP offers an exciting, but very general vision for learning and teaching, lifelong and lifewide. Based on its discussion, I believe we now have the necessary infrastructure for an innovative twenty-first century model of K-20 education to replace the now obsolete industrial-era schools and campuses developed in response to a shift from agricultural to industrial society (Dede, 2010). However, one's view of educational improvement can be evolutionary rather than transformative and still benefit from the NETP's analysis of the developments above and their larger policy context.

Given the situation described above, this volume about *Breakthrough Teaching and Learning* is a very important contribution in understanding how to apply emerging technologies to particular aspects of learning and teaching. Sweeping, but general syntheses like the NETP have value only if supplemented by thoughtful, detailed analyses of how specific types of learners can benefit from the new models of instruction, assessment, and links between school and community that sophisticated interactive media enable. This book provides such a focused, reflective perspective on students with diverse learning needs who find little benefit in conventional, presentational, print-based instruction.

The seven chapters address different dimensions of this challenge.

1. *Converging Trends in Educational and Assistive Technology* provides an introductory view of technology in education to set the stage for the chapters that follow. Drawing from national survey data, the authors find that, while technology is found in every school and nearly every teenager's pocket it is not being leveraged as a learning tool as often as one might hope.

2. *The Power of Social Networking for Professional Development* examines the ways in which participation in social networking sites not only promotes resource sharing among educators, but also contributes to personalized professional development.

3. *What Can Technology Learn from the Brain?* explores what new insights technology developers and educators can gain into the teaching and learning processes from scientific breakthroughs in understanding the cognitive role of delusions, mirror neurons, anxiety, and reciprocal feedback.

4. *The Potential of Social Media for Students with Disabilities* presents an overview of how and why social media are used around the world by children and teens with an examination of the potential of social media for students with disabilities.

5. *Exergames Get Kids Moving* explores how active gaming or exergaming can assist individuals with disabilities to become more active, gain motor skills, and enjoy a more inclusive gaming experience.

6. *Personalizing Assessment* provides an overview of the potential for technology-enhanced assessment practice that makes possible a personalization approach.

7. *Exploring the Minds of Innovators* explores the minds of innovators across a number of disciplines: people who have changed the game, made breakthroughs, and implemented changes resulting in new approaches that make a difference in education and technology development.

References

Bjerede, M., Atkins, K., & Dede, C. (2010). Ubiquitous mobile technologies and the transformation of schooling. *Educational Technology, 50*(2), 3–7.

Dede, C. (2008, May/June). A seismic shift in epistemology. *EDUCAUSE Review, 43*(3), 80–81.

Dede, C. (2009). Immersive interfaces for engagement and learning. *Science, 323*(5910), 66–69.

Dede, C. (2010). Commentary: Transforming schooling via the 2010 National Educational Technology Plan. *Teachers College Record*. Published: 2.06.10. ID Number: 15998. Accessed May 6, 2010, from http://www.tcrecord.org at 1:11:52 PM.

U.S. Department of Education. (2010). *2010 National Educational Technology Plan*. http://www.ed.gov/technology/netp-2010.

Converging Trends in Educational and Assistive Technology

Tracy Gray, Heidi Silver-Pacuilla, Alise Brann, Cynthia Overton, and Rebecca Reynolds

Setting the Stage

The work of the National Center for Technology Innovation supports the notion that all students can benefit from accessible and assistive technology (AT) and the ways these tools can promote learning. This chapter provides an overview of the trends in technology for education and the diverse learning needs of students in classrooms throughout the nation. This convergence of trends illuminates the essential role of technology in education, especially for students who struggle or who are disengaged from academic success.

This chapter offers and introductory view of technology in education to set the stage for the chapters that follow. Drawing from national survey data, we find that while technology is found in every school and nearly every teenager's pocket, it is not being leveraged as a learning tool as often as one might hope.

We begin with an examination of trends in technology development and utilization in educational and consumer environments, and those related to policy and philanthropic investments. Building on the framework provided by the 2010 National Education Technology Plan (NETP), we explore how technology can be integrated in schools to support teaching and learning, assessment, productivity, and infrastructure. The next section looks at the diverse needs of our student population and innovative ways that technologies can be leveraged to personalize the learning experience. The chapter concludes with a call for personalization and connected teaching to ensure that all students reach their academic and social potential.

T. Gray (✉)
American Institutes for Research, Washington, DC, USA
e-mail: tgray@air.org

T. Gray and H. Silver-Pacuilla (eds.), *Breakthrough Teaching and Learning:*
How Educational and Assistive Technologies are Driving Innovation,
DOI 10.1007/978-1-4419-7768-7_2, © Springer Science+Business Media, LLC 2011

A Short Look Back

Currently, the U.S. educational landscape reflects the infusion of technology into nearly every aspect of school life. Major changes are evident over the past 5 years in how technology is viewed and deployed in the classroom in terms of infrastructure, equipment, online learning, teacher training, and policies.

Awareness of how technology could accommodate students with special needs has gained traction in the past 5 years as assistive technologies increasingly look and function like mainstream educational or consumer technologies. More devices and online applications were being built with accessibility and customizable features making them usable by individuals with disabilities (Gray, Silver-Pacuilla, Overton, & Brann, 2010). Principles of universal design for learning (UDL) were embraced by more educators as they aimed to differentiate instruction and ensure the academic success of all students, particularly those underperforming on high-profile state tests.

Throughout the USA, education has become increasingly entwined with the digital consumer landscape. We are no longer asking *whether* digital materials and tools should be integrated into teaching and learning, but *how*, *how well*, and *under what conditions* do they meet students' needs.

The Students' World

Meanwhile, the students' world has experienced dramatic change as well, with technology permeating nearly every aspect of daily life, often in ways that is unique to tweens and teens. The always-wired generation has left teachers and parents scrambling to imagine ways to engage students and enhance learning in the classroom. A window into the world of young people reveals:

- *Gaming* saturated the youth culture with 97% of students reporting playing regularly (Lemke, Coughlin, & Reifsneider, 2009; Lenhart, Arafeh, Smith, & Macgill, 2008), and games of all sorts being tried in instruction to engage students and to teach them such vital skills as teamwork, decision-making, and digital literacy (Chandler, 2009; Van Horn, 2007).
- *Social media* sites as a means for socializing and collaboration (Lenhart, Madden, Rankin-Macgill, & Smith, 2007) became so integral in the lives of tweens and teens that 96% of students with Internet access reported engaging in social networking and spending as much or more time online than watching television (National School Boards, 2007). More than 67% of teens with their own social network page say they update their page at least once a week (Nielsen, 2009).
- *Text messaging* became one of the more popular pastimes internationally, with the average number of texts sent and received by teens increasing 566% in 2 years (Nielsen, 2009). By late 2009, texting had taken over as the most popular form of communication among teenagers, surpassing email, instant messaging, social networking, and face-to-face communication (Lenhart, Ling, Campbell,

& Purcell, 2010). One-third of teenagers who text daily report sending more than 100 texts per day, while 15% send in excess of 200 texts a day (Lenhart et al., 2010).

- *Portable media devices* have become ubiquitous. Three-quarters of teens 12–17 years old now own a cell phone, a sharp increase from 2004 where 45% of the teens in the same age group owned cell phones (Lenhart et al., 2010). In addition, children began to have access to these devices at younger ages with 93% of children aged 6–9 years old living in homes with a cell phone, half with their own portable video game player, and a third with their own cell phone (Shuler, 2009).
- *Cell phones* and portable media devices have helped bridge the digital divide, providing greater access to online content to many individuals without a home computer. In households making more than $30,000 per year, 92% had access to a computer in the home, compared to 70% of households making less than $30,000 per year. Among low-income teens, 41% use their cell phones to go online (Lenhart et al., 2010).

The youth of today are clearly wired and tech-savvy. The Pew Research Center (2010) released a report on "millennials," individuals who were 18–29 in 2010. In response to the question, *What makes your generation unique?*, 24% identified technology as the most important factor. This statement, in conjunction with the other factors, led the researchers to label the millennials as "confident, connected, and open to change." The Joan Gantz Cooney Center studied younger children and found their use of media and media access devices nearly ever present, leading many to conclude that the potential for mobile learning is nearly limitless.

Despite the potential benefits of mobile learning technologies, many educators view cell phones as disruptive elements in the classroom; 24% of teens report that their schools ban cell phones entirely (Lenhart et al., 2010). However, of the students attending schools with cell phone bans, a substantial majority (65%) still bring their phones with them every day (Lenhart et al.). *Pockets of Potential* (Shuler, 2009) encourages educators to consider how to keep children learning and creating in and out of the school day. At the end of the decade, a growing number of parents, educators, and public policymakers increased the call for integrating technology into teaching and for learning to improve the acquisition of knowledge, enhance social skills, and strengthen students' ability to express themselves (Ito et al., 2008; National School Boards, 2007).

Zhao and Qiu (this volume) explore the social implications behind these numbers from a global perspective and what these tools mean in the lives of students with disabilities. As we demonstrate later in the chapter, students and teachers both are using technology in their personal lives *more often* and *in more ways* than at school.

Major Policy Initiatives

With the continued proliferation of these technology tools and their early adoption by young people, we are challenged to unleash the power of technology and digital media for teaching and learning. The authors in this book make clear that no government agency, organization, or program can meet these challenges alone. Rather, it will require a coordinated effort by educators, researchers, business leaders, technology innovators, policymakers, and parent groups. The key to change will be broad public engagement at all levels.

Since 2009, there has been a significant shift in public policies and standards that have pushed assistive and accessible technologies for individuals with disabilities to the forefront of the national agenda. The American Recovery and Reinvestment Act (ARRA) of 2009 initially provided more than $100 billion to education-related efforts that included funds to address the needs of students with disabilities within the stated priorities:

- Make progress toward the establishment of research-based rigorous standards and assessments, particularly for students with disabilities and English language learners
- Provide support for the lowest performing schools to ensure that students have access to a quality education
- Improve the quality of teacher effectiveness, including the development of teacher performance assessment tools
- Establish reliable data systems to track student progress and foster continuous improvement

As a part of the ARRA funds, the U.S. Department of Education established two new competitive funding streams with the goal of fostering innovation: Race to the Top (RttT) with a budget of $4 billion and the Investing in Innovation Fund (i3) with a budget of $650 million. RttT was established as a competitive grant program to encourage and reward states that are implementing significant reforms in the four priority areas. To increase their odds for winning a grant, many states passed significant educational reform laws that mandated the development of more charter schools and tightened teacher accountability and tenure requirements. These are considered important by the Obama Administration but remain controversial with many teacher unions throughout the nation.

The i3 initiative was established to provide competitive grants to applicants with a record of improving student achievement in order to expand the implementation of, and investment in, innovative practices that are demonstrated to have an impact on (1) improving student achievement or student growth for high-need students and (2) promoting school readiness, closing achievement gaps, decreasing dropout rates, increasing high-school graduation rates, and improving teacher and school leader effectiveness. A total of 1,669 applications were received for the first round of funding seeking $50 million "scale-up" grants, $30 million "validation" grants, or $5 million "development" grants.

The tension between the call for evidence-based practices and the potential to engage students through the use of technology, particularly those with special needs, surfaces throughout the policy initiatives of the Obama Administration. For example, a review of the NETP (March, 2010) calls for major investments to address barriers to educational technology innovation such as poor infrastructure and professional development. The 114-page document reveals an intent not only to integrate technology throughout the curriculum (and beyond), but also to implement some major – some might say radical – changes to education itself.

Some of the assumptions questioned in the NETP are basic to public education, including age-determined grade levels, measuring achievement through "seat time," keeping students in the same classes throughout the year, and keeping academic disciplines separate. The Plan advocates tighter integration between K-12 and higher education, and advocates for more collaboration between secondary and postsecondary institutions.

In an effort to deepen the research base for the use of technology for learning, legislation was passed to establish the National Center for Research in Advanced Information and Digital Technologies, more than 10 years in the making. The purpose of the Center is to support a comprehensive research and development program to "harness the increasing capability of advanced information and digital technologies to improve all levels of learning and education, formal and informal, in order to provide Americans with the knowledge and skills needed to compete in the global economy" (see http://digitalpromise.org/Files/Digital-Promise-Press-Release.pdf). Authorized in 2008 by amendments to the Higher Education Act (HEA) of 2008 (PL 110-315) and funded initially by the U.S. Department of Education, the Center intends to support the research needed to understand how best to integrate technology for formal and informal teaching and learning, and to work closely with the goals of the NETP.

Following on the heels of the NETP, the Obama Administration released its "Blueprint for Reform" for the reauthorization of the Elementary and Secondary Education Act. The law, currently known as the No Child Left Behind Act (NCLB), has been due for reauthorization since 2007. The blueprint builds upon the principles laid out with the release of the ARRA funds and offers the first step in the development of legislation for the reauthorization of NCLB. This marks the most significant undertaking in the realm of federal education policy since the law was originally mandated in 2001. The Blueprint calls for less emphasis on test scores and more on student attainment of a broad base of knowledge, increasing high-school graduation rates, and ensuring that graduates are prepared for college and the workplace. It calls for rigorous common standards and revises the accountability structure to reward schools, districts, and states that make steady progress in increasing student activity. It offers districts' flexibility in spending funds on human capital development in exchange for long overdue reforms to teacher and principal evaluation systems. The Blueprint places particular emphasis on the inclusion of students with special needs. It calls for better teacher preparation to address the needs of students with disabilities and tests that more accurately access student abilities.

In March 2010, the Federal Communications Commission (FCC) submitted The National Broadband Plan (http://www.broadband.gov/plan) to Congress. This ambitious plan represents a critical step in the progress of accessible technology policy. With this effort, the FCC seeks to ensure that every American has access to an affordable national broadband network, including high-speed voice, data, and video communications, and emergency and entertainment infrastructure. The plan includes a detailed set of policy recommendations and strategies for how this goal would be reached with the greatest degree of efficiency and affordability. Likening broadband to electricity, the executive summary calls the technology "a foundation for economic growth, job creation, global competitiveness, and a better way of life" (U.S. Federal Communications Commission, pg.1). There are four key points outlined in the plan:

1. Design policies to ensure competition
2. Ensure efficiency in asset management and allocations
3. Reform current deployment services in high-cost areas
4. Reform policies to maximize the benefits of broadband when used in public sectors like education, health care, and government

The call for a comprehensive vision for broadband reform and accessibility in public sectors is particularly acute considering the latest data from the FCC that only 42% of people with disabilities have high-speed Internet services at home and 39% of all nonadopters have disabilities (Lyle, 2010). To address the continued disparity of broadband use, the FCC is mandating the application of existing federal telecommunication requirements to Internet-based mobile and other technologies, the wider availability of video description, the need for more relevant emergency information access requirements, and the critical necessity for video programming devices and program menus to be accessible by individuals with disabilities, particularly those who experience loss of vision. While the exact parameters of the FCC's authority to issue regulations to accomplish these objectives remains in dispute at this writing, the gravitas of the Commission to back the objectives has already begun to shape industry and community responses.

Major Philanthropic Initiatives

Concomitant with the significant increase in public policy mandates is the growing number of philanthropic initiatives that support research and innovation to expand our knowledge base of the important role of technology to engage the digital learner. The challenge for educators is to identify ways to harness our students' passion and comfort with technology tools throughout the learning experience with the goal of heightening student engagement and participation. A growing number of foundations have provided support to identify ways to foster this type of innovation in the classroom. More specifically, the MacArthur Foundation, with an investment of $1.7 million, established the Digital Media and Learning initiative in 2007 to provide an understanding of how digital media are changing the way young people learn, play, socialize, and participate in civic life. In 2010, the Foundation made ten awards to innovators who will deploy games, mobile phone applications, virtual worlds, and social networks to create the learning laboratories of the twenty-first century. Winners include a project to show youth-produced videos on 2,200 Los Angeles city buses; the next generation of a graphical programming language that allows young people to create their own interactive stories, games, and animations; and an online game that teaches youth the environmental impact of their personal choices.

Other foundations have made investments in technology, media, and innovation including the Knight Foundation, which funds the Knight Community Information Challenge, a 5-year, $24 million initiative to help local foundations support creative ways to use new media and technology to engage communities. The Robert Wood Johnson Foundation (RWJF) has established the Games for Health program through a grant of $8.25 million to build on the ongoing work to understand the potential for games to improve health and health care and to forge connections between the games and health fields. Yang and Foley (this volume) explore this initiative in their chapter, "Exergames Get Kids Moving."

In an effort to leverage their funding resources, a dozen foundations established a collaboration to provide support for the selected winners of the U.S. Department of Education's i3 Fund. This unique fund would provide up to $506 billion in 2010, to match federal grants intended to foster education reform. This commitment will provide support and leverage to meet the required 20% private match serve for winning proposals. The collaboration includes: the Annie E. Casey Foundation; the Bill & Melinda Gates Foundation; the Carnegie Corporation of New York; the Charles Stewart Mott Foundation; the Ford Foundation; the John D. & Catherine T. MacArthur Foundation; the Lumina Foundation; the Robertson Foundation; the Wallace Foundation; the Walton Family Foundation; the William & Flora Hewlett Foundation; and the W.K. Kellogg Foundation. Further, this collaborative effort will establish an online portal that will allow applicants to apply for matching funds from all the foundations in one step, streamlining the task of seeking money from multiple sources. The Web site, Foundation Registry i3 (http://foundationregistryi3.org/), will simplify the private-funding application process and increase access and visibility for applicants.

Educational Technology in Schools

As noted earlier, the NETP presents a model of twenty-first century learning powered by technology, with goals and recommendations in five essential areas: learning, assessment, teaching, infrastructure, and productivity. The Plan also identifies a set of "grand challenge problems" that should be funded and coordinated at the national level: establishing an integrated end-to-end real-time system for managing learning outcomes and costs across our education system at all levels.

The emphasis toward personalized learning and connected teaching is described in the NETP as a teaching model in which "teams of connected educators replace solo practitioners and classrooms are fully connected to provide educators with 24/7 access to data and analytic tools as well as to resources that help them act on the insights the data provide" (NETP, p. viii). This model has the potential to create an inclusive technology-supported education that can deliver benefits to all students, their teachers, and families. However, there is a disconnect between the aims of the NETP and the realities of present-day teaching and learning, and the technology infrastructure, including hardware, software, and connectivity in schools. The data indicate that technology is becoming a growing presence in today's schools, inching us closer to some of the goals of the NETP, but not in a coordinated or systematic way. In this section, we contrast the NETP goals with some of the latest statistics and trends on teaching, learning, assessment, productivity, and infrastructure.

Teaching

According to a new report released by the U.S. Department of Education (Gray, Thomas, & Lewis, 2010), as of fall 2008, every single public school in the country is using computing technology in some way as part of instruction and every school has at least one instructional computer with Internet access.

Teachers report that they use technology for five key tasks including: teaching and instruction, preparing for instruction, data-driven decision-making, and their own learning, collaboration, and professional development. As for one-to-many instruction, the survey measured the availability of different teaching technologies for the classroom, finding that interactive whiteboards saw significant penetration, with 73% of schools reporting deployments. Videoconferencing systems were installed in 22% of schools, and video cameras were in 93% of schools. The study does not report teachers' frequency of use of these technologies, nor does it discuss the how much time teachers spend in training to use technology.

The presence of technology as a teaching tool in the hands of educators is only one side of the issue when it comes to technology integration. Another important role that technology tools play in schools is to promote productive inquiry and constructive project-based work, resulting in increased student engagement. Many researchers in the field of educational technology and the learning sciences are investigating the development, implementation, and outcomes of students' use of software, Web-based educational services, and online learning programs that are being offered nationwide. These learning opportunities take many forms, ranging from informal to formal settings, offered in school for credit as well as after-school programs. They use a variety of models that include various degrees of online learning combined with face-to-face interactions. Such opportunities are now even expanding in some states to include entirely online models of distance learning offered to students at all grade levels to work and learn remotely. The availability of such opportunities for U.S. students, however, is far from being either uniform or diffuse.

As for the technology infrastructure in schools, desktop computers are the most prevalent (76%); and 58% of schools had laptops on carts as of fall 2008 (Gray, Thomas, et al., 2010). While 78% of public schools reported having some form of wireless network on campus, only 39% said their wireless access was available across the entire campus. Another 30% said wireless was available in only part of the school, and 9% said their wireless connections extended only from a laptop to a cart, with the cart plugged into a wired port in a wall. While many teachers report using digital media tools (66%), digital resources (46%), and games (42%), they also report that they are lacking access to mobile computers or devices for every student, and consistent, reliable, Internet access in their classrooms.

Teacher perceptions of training and the use of educational technology indicated differences depending on the level of poverty concentration in a school (Gray, Thomas, et al., 2010). For example, a larger percentage of teachers in more affluent areas than those who work in high-poverty districts agreed that teachers are sufficiently trained in technology usage (74% versus 62%), teachers are sufficiently trained in technology implementations (67% versus 56%), technical support for educational technology is adequate (74% versus 60%), and funding for educational technology is being spent in the most appropriate ways (79% versus 69%). It appears from these data that the problems of the socioeconomic digital divide are mirrored not only in the home setting, but also within the school.

Overall, the ratio of students to instructional computers with Internet access was 3:1 (Gray, Thomas, et al., 2010). While the ratio of students to computers sounds fairly promising, and while the report indicates that a full 91% of computers in public schools were used for instruction (and almost all of them – 98% – had Internet access), the study does not distinguish whether this "instruction" reflects one-to-many use by the teacher or constructive use by the student (one-to-one). Further, the study does not address specifics as to *the extent to which* and *how* teachers and students are using technology for learning in their daily lives within the school setting.

Learning

To better understand the *ways* in which teachers and students in U.S. schools are using technology, between October and December 2009, the nonprofit organization Project Tomorrow conducted its annual survey. It elicited responses from 1,987 future teachers currently in teacher training, 38,642 in-service teachers, and 3,890 principals. They also published a complementary online survey of 299,677 K-12 students and 26,312 parents. On the whole, the results position students as a population who are primed and eager for technology-based learning opportunities, and school administrators as people who readily see the potential and promote the benefits of technology, teachers, however, come across as a population with mixed opinions and perceptions of the utility, feasibility, and benefits of integrating technology for teaching and learning.

Students are increasingly taking responsibility for their own learning, defining their own education path through alternative sources, and feeling a responsibility for creating personalized learning experiences. The survey of students (Project Tomorrow, 2010) found that:

- Close to 65% of students in grades 9–12 *communicate* with other students using technology for schoolwork; 51% of 6–8 graders and about 12% of those in grades 3–5 use technology for this purpose.
- Close to 50% of students in grades 9–12 use social media tools to *collaborate* for schoolwork; 34% of 6–8 graders use technology for this purpose.

The technology-based activities engaged by students include: playing online games or simulations; tutoring others and seeking help via social network; taking tests online; completing writing assignments; turning in papers for plagiarism checks; creating slide shows, videos, or Web pages; using online text books; and uploading assignments to the school portal. These findings support the claim that students are developing their skills as "free agent learners," adept at choosing from available tools for multiple personal and school-based activities (Christensen, Horn, & Johnson, 2008; Project Tomorrow, 2010). Yet students consistently report that a perceived lack of sophisticated use of emerging technology tools in schools is holding back their education and contributing to their disengagement.

Overall, this survey data confirm that teaching and learning throughout the nation remain delivered through traditional, large group instruction and individual learning in the core content areas. Technology innovators and evaluators have not made clear the ways in which the array of technological tools can enrich and improve teaching and learning. Witness the recent critiques that reveal the widespread use of interactive whiteboards as simply another teacher-controlled blackboard in the classroom (McCrummen, 2010). The critical question that we must address is how to bridge the distance between the vision offered by the NETP and the realities of schools today.

Assessment

Meanwhile, as anyone involved in American education through the implementation of the No Child Left Behind Act of 2001 can attest, assessment policy matters. The accountability system put into place by the Act, including the threat of negative consequences, created a significant shift in the priorities placed on standardized tests and the performance of students and schools. Some groups were included in state tests for the first time ever. The performance of groups whose tests scores were reported as "disaggregated groups" – language minorities, students with disabilities, racial, and ethnic groups – was suddenly thrust into public debate. Advocacy groups cheered the newly available data that illustrated the "achievement gap" they had been documenting for years: even as overall scores had improved for schools, districts, and states, the performance of subgroups was often stagnant or, at best, not keeping pace with the majority of students and was, in fact, widening through the end of the last century (Artiles & Bal, 2008; García & Guerra, 2004). The inclusion of these students in school performance profiles made clear the need for more inclusive assessments and testing practices. As a result, more attention has been paid through the past decade to document the efficacy of accommodations and alternate forms of assessments.

The NETP calls for smarter assessment systems which require the innovative use of technology to create the "instrumented classroom" (U.S. Department of Education Office of Educational Technology 2010). The technology-based assessments envisioned in the NETP are systems that align with learning to offer formative and diagnostic data for instructional decisions. These systems would represent a new generation of tests that offer adapted versions of test items, require constructive responses to real-world type test items, and would be aligned to standards and curriculum sequences in order to suggest instructional plans. This vision is far from reality in most states and districts which are only now completing a full implementation of standardized one-size-fits-all type of testing protocol with accommodations made on individual basis.

Russell (this volume), in the chapter *Personalizing Assessment* could be universally designed so that all students can demonstrate what they know, without the need for time- and resource-intensive accommodations.

Productivity

Great potential can also be found in utilizing technology to coordinate administrative processes throughout the field of education. The NETP suggests drawing on productivity technology for measuring and managing costs, using data in decision-making, employing iterative design and development, reorganizing teaching and learning, and extending learning time.

Productivity software can be especially beneficial when managing the needs of students with disabilities. Although paper-based individual education plans (IEPs) are still prevalent throughout local education agencies in the USA, developers of electronic IEP software are quick to note features offered through their systems, including Medicaid claim capabilities; a data bank of IEP goals, objectives, and benchmarks; and language translation to better engage parents who are not fluent in English (Serfass & Peterson, 2007). Furthermore, electronic IEPs that align with a district's student information system enhance access to information needed for the IEP process, such as grades, attendance records, test scores, and discipline information (THE Journal, 2008). Such features can make the IEP process and monitoring more efficient, saving teachers valuable time which can be redirected toward pressing needs of the students they serve. Furthermore, many of the features of electronic IEPs serve as safeguards to errors and the exclusion of information, thus increasing the likelihood that schools and districts stay in compliance with the law. Technology can also be used to support the IEP process by tracking a district's assistive technology inventory to inform purchasing needs for students who require such support.

Productivity tools that support data-driven decision-making have also received significant attention. Public schools reported that they used their district network or the Internet to provide standardized assessment results and data for teachers to individualize instruction (87%), to inform instructional planning at the school (85%), online student assessment (72%), and high-quality digital content (65%) (Gray, Thomas, et al., 2010). The study does not indicate the extent to which teachers use technology and the Internet to help prepare lessons or to engage in ongoing professional development opportunities.

As suggested in the NETP, productivity technology should be used to organize efforts of an entire system to help relevant stakeholders work together in the best interest of the students they serve. However, while software vendors offer information on their respective IEP software, little objective information is available to education professionals on identifying IEP management systems that would best address their needs. More objective research and reviews of these software packages would help district personnel be more informed consumers.

Infrastructure

Expanding and enhancing schools' and districts' infrastructure for technology use is another major component of the NETP. One of the stated goals of the NETP is: "All students and educators will have access to a comprehensive infrastructure for learning when and where they need it" (p. 51). The reality of school capacity as outlined above indicates the need for help to ensure that equipment is functioning, regularly updated, and supported; teachers are trained to use what is available; and systems are interoperable. The NETP recognizes that these issues are negatively impacting the effective use of technology for teaching and learning.

Recommendations in the Plan in the Infrastructure section reflect the need to pay attention to capacity building – equipment, broadband access, software, open source content, and human expertise. The Plan also acknowledges the need to address outdated policies that are creating barriers, such as the restrictions in the eRate program on Internet safety and school network security. The eRate program has had a significant impact on making technology equipment and Internet access available to schools since it was enacted in 1998, but outdated regulations are hampering schools' efforts to adopt new models of service delivery, such as allowing students to access the school network through their own devices (*Sources: E-Rate Overview:* http://www.universalservice.org/sl/about/overview-program.aspx cited in NETP, p. 55).

The Plan recognizes that "effective process redesign within school systems will require close coordination among all these functions" (p. 60). The imperative for teamwork to address infrastructure issues of access, interoperability, support, and implementation has long been a theme in the training for assistive technology implementation. Nationally recognized groups such as the Quality Indicators for AT (QIAT: http://natri.uky.edu/assoc_projects/qiat/) and the National Center on Accessible Instructional Materials (AIM) Consortium (http://aim.cast.org/) have long maintained the importance of teams and processes that will sustain high-quality implementation of accessible and assistive technology for students.

Struggling Student Trends and Statistics

Several national indicators clearly document that there are many struggling students for whom teaching and learning as usual is not meeting their needs. This section provides the key indicators to understand the numbers for struggling students, be they those with diagnosed disabilities, chronic health concerns, general disengagement, or others who are not succeeding in the current curriculum. Although English language learners represent a large and growing population in our schools, the role of technology to support their learning is beyond the scope of this chapter. There is a growing body of evidence that underscores the critical role that technology can play with these struggling students, but the practices and research are still emerging.

One indicator of struggling students is a continued high rate of noncompletion from high school. While the national dropout rate is decreasing, it remains at an unacceptably high rate, particularly among certain groups of students. Nearly one in four students fails to graduate from high school on time. Low-income students drop out of school at rates ten times higher than middle- and high-income peers. Hispanic students born in the USA have dropout rates that hover around 11%; that rate is closer to 35% for Hispanic students who are foreign-born (Cataldi, Laird, & KewalRamani, 2009). Nearly 44% of students receiving special education services for emotional disabilities drop out of school before completion, and 28% of special education students of all categories do not complete high school (National Longitudinal Transition Study – 2, 2005).

How is technology being used to address this issue? Results from a recent national survey of K-12 districts indicate that 75% of U.S. districts have students enrolled in online courses and that the number of K-12 students engaged in online courses in 2007–2008 was over one million (Picciano & Seaman, 2009). Credit recovery, or re-taking classes which were failed, is one of the most common applications of online courses; more than half of respondents from another national survey of administrators from 2,500 school districts reported using online learning in their schools for credit recovery, with just over a fifth (22%) reporting "wide use" of online learning for this purpose (Greaves & Hayes, 2008; Watson & Gemin, 2008). Even school systems not integrating online learning in a systematic way are finding such online learning alternatives appealing to otherwise disengaged struggling teens.

Today, special education in the nation is facing new challenges and opportunities. Federal law governing special education, the Individuals with Disabilities Educational Improvement Act (IDEA) as reauthorized in 2004 with regulations released in 2006, brought several of the current policies into the forefront of educational practice.

- Response to Intervention (RTI) quickly gained popular support as a school-wide approach to disability identification and reduction by more deliberate, diagnostic instruction, particularly for early reading and mathematics (see the National Center on RTI, http://www.rti4success.org/). Effective management of the data collection and analysis necessary to coordinate RTI can be supported by productivity software and data visualization displays.
- Universal Design for Learning (UDL) was codified into law as an approach that could accommodate diverse learners within the general classroom and curriculum. Its core principles of providing for multiple means of expression, reception, presentation, and assessment rely heavily on technology for teacher productivity and adaptable instructional materials.

- The National Instructional Materials Accessibility Standard (NIMAS: http://aim.cast.org/) was included in the 2006 IDEA regulations, requiring publishers of instructional materials to provide source files to a repository from which schools could deliver them to students with print disabilities in a variety of formats. These formats are all managed with technology, and many of the student-ready versions are digital, requiring devices or Internet access to use.
- The directive to include students in the general education classroom and be taught with the general curriculum to the greatest extent possible begins the transfers of responsibility for special education services for the majority of students to the general education teacher, in collaboration with a special educator.

These trends are shifting the way special education is planned and delivered and how students are classified and served. As the NETP points out, NIMAS represents a paradigm shift in how disabilities are recognized and accommodated:

> The dramatic effect of the NIMAS legislation is not really in the technology itself, but in the change in how we think about diversity that the technology promotes. The conceptual shift is evident in that Congress calls for schools to provide alternative versions for all students who have "print disabilities." In that remarkable wording shift, "learning disabilities" to "print disabilities," lies a profound alteration in the response to diversity and disability. By recognizing that many learning problems are resident not just in the child but in the medium of instruction, the NIMAS legislation also recognizes that the limits of print are too costly for American education. Printed textbooks cannot adequately meet the challenge of diversity, and we will need to shift our educational practices to new technologies that – through more universal designs – are equitable and effective for all of our learners.

Indeed as educational and assistive technologies merge and general and special education "blur" (Fuchs, Fuchs, & Stecker, 2010), the distinctions are increasingly difficult to make. The most recent data representing 2006–2007 (http://www.ideadata.org) show that special education services were provided to 7.7% of school children or 6.1 million students. Over 57% of them spent more than 80% of their school day in the general education classroom. High-incidence disability groups (such as students with learning disabilities, communication or speech-language disorders, and other health impairments, which include chronic diseases and Attention Deficit Hyperactivity Disorder) are leading this trend toward inclusion, many of them served 100% of the time in the general classroom. A recent example of this convergence is the decision by the Chancellor of the New York City schools to dismantle special education programs and mainstream the majority of students into general education classrooms and schools.

While every student served under IDEA is eligible for the consideration of assistive technology which could support their achievement and independence, the rate at which AT is actually delivered and supported for children is inconsistent and not well-documented. A small survey ($n=628$) of AT use provided data to describe students using AT by grade level, disability category, sex, ethnicity, and placement in the school (general education class, special education class, alternative school, etc.) (Quinn, Behrmann, Mastriopieri, & Chung, 2009). Those with multiple disabilities were reported as using AT most frequently (27.7%), followed by students with learning disabilities (16.7%) and orthopedic impairments (14.6%). Students were more likely to use AT in self-contained special education classrooms (40.4%) and resource rooms (19%) than in general education classrooms (11.5%) or at home (2.3%). Such low utilization is echoed in studies of students with visual impairments which estimate that only 40% of students are learning with technology in schools (Kapperman, Sticken, & Heinze, 2002; Kelly, 2008) or studies of students with learning disabilities that estimate 25–35% are learning with technology (Cortiella, 2009).

Meanwhile, the national survey on children, with special health care needs (CSHCN), documents those children who require above-routine health and related services for ongoing physical, emotional, behavioral, or developmental conditions. From this dataset, it is estimated that 10.2 million children have such needs (U.S. Department of Health and Human Services, Health Resources and Services Administration, Maternal and Child Bureau, 2007). Researchers estimate that 13–20% of all children (Bethell, Read, Blumberg, & Newacheck, 2008) and an estimated 16.8% of adolescents aged 12–17 have a special health care need (Mulye et al., 2009). Children with these conditions may or may not be receiving special education services, clinical therapy, or assistive technology devices or services.

Some of the fastest growing childhood special health conditions include autism, attention disorders, obesity, diabetes, and asthma. Specifically, autism and Autism Spectrum Disorders (ASD) is the fastest growing special education category. From the 1992–1993 to 2001–2002 school years, data indicate an expansion of 528% and an annual average growth of 22.7% in this category (Safran, 2008). It is estimated that ASD impacts one of every 150 U.S. children (Centers for Disease Control and Prevention, 2007). Attention Deficit Hyperactivity Disorder (ADHD) affects an estimated 8.8% of U.S. children aged 6 through 17 (CDC, 2003), and it is often diagnosed as a co-occurring condition with other health or learning conditions. Children with ADHD now constitute the majority of the special education catego-ries of Other Health Impaired and Emotional Disturbance and substantial propor-tions of the Learning Disability and Mental Retardation categories. Many other children with ADHD are served under Section 504 plans and spend their day in general education classrooms (Schnoes, Reid, Wagner, & Marder, 2006, p. 494). How active gaming or exergames could benefit the health of these children is explored in Yang and Foley (this volume).

From the CSHCN dataset, the need for and provision of assistive technology devices and services to address impairments and needs are also documented. Benedict and Baumgardner (2009) estimate that 49% of children with special health care needs require AT and AT services, defined in the dataset as vision or hearing aids or care, communication or mobility devices, or other medical equip-ment. From the same survey, *unmet needs* for AT among CSHCN were reported at 25% of children requiring communication aids or devices, 9% of children requiring hearing aids, and 9% of those requiring mobility aids or devices. In fact, the researchers state that "in the U.S., identification as having special educational needs does not give children an advantage in term of access to AT" (p. 589).

Clearly, there is an unacceptable rate of unmet need for AT, whether for access, independence, or learning. And while educational and assistive technology con-tinue to converge and general and special education continue to merge, the diversity of students' needs is increasing. Accessible, assistive, and universally designed technology available in all learning environments is as important as ever, especially if we are to personalize learning.

The State of Assistive Technology

The Horizon Report (Johnson, Smith, Levine, & Haywood, 2010) highlights consumer technology development trends that will impact teaching and learning in the next 5 years: cloud computing, collaborative environments, game-based learning, mobile devices, augmented reality, and flexible displays. As we have described before, the convergence of general and special education services mirrors the convergence of consumer and assistive technologies.

In an effort to better understand what it means to be state of the art in the area of assistive technology and help practitioners identify such devices, NCTI contacted stakeholders in the educational and assistive technology fields to gather their perspectives. More than 100 professionals representing a broad range of sectors – education and training; academia; business and industry; federal, state, and local governments; and professional education or AT associations – offered their perspectives. An analysis of the data revealed five themes defining state-of-the-art AT, including

1. Convergence of tools
2. Customizability and UDL
3. Portability for independence
4. Research or evidence-based
5. Interoperability

NCTI drew on respondents' feedback to define each of these themes and identify specific examples (Gray, Silver-Pacuilla, et al., 2010) which are summarized below.

Convergence is defined as the transformation of various systems or devices into a single platform. Several respondents pointed to handheld communication devices such as smart phones to illustrate converged platforms. This is because in addition to serving as a means of communication, smart phones have the capability to run multiple applications (apps) that support and accompany students throughout the day. The use of apps is widespread, with over one billion downloaded to date (Pew Research Center, 2010). Furthermore, with 47% of the top selling apps targeting preschool or elementary aged children, clearly future educational possibilities are growing.

Customizability and UDL are associated with devices designed to be flexible enough to be configured to meet the unique needs of individuals. These characteristics in mainstream technology are especially important so that few students with disabilities are provided personal AT as described above. Customizable design features that can meet the needs of multiple users are becoming increasingly prevalent in the gaming industry. This industry has captured the teenage market, with 97% of adolescents between the ages of 12 and 17 playing video games. Games are associated with better cognitive, skill-based, and affective outcomes (Lemke et al., 2009), presenting an ideal opportunity for educators to tap into students' recreational interests to promote learning. Organizations such as the Serious Games Initiative have made great effort to draw attention to the educational, social, and health benefits of digital games for students with and without disabilities.

Research and evidence on AT demonstrates the utility, interest, and efficacy of a product. Understanding such information helps educators understand what to expect of devices they consider incorporating into instructional practices for students with disabilities. Great opportunity exists in the field to engage in AT-related research. However, one challenge to state-of-the-art AT research is that assistive devices have not always kept up with the latest technologies as seen in consumer electronic devices that offer a wide range of options (e.g., wireless access and Bluetooth). In some cases, AT developers have been discouraged from incorporating new features because of funding and implementation environment mandates, and an effort to keep end users from being overwhelmed. Consequently, research that provides information on which features are most effective for which populations, under which conditions, and for which tasks is still in the early stages for AT. NCTI supports the call by the FCC's Broadband Plan to reverse Medicare and Medicaid rules that deny coverage of multi-tasking devices and would consider this as a major driver of innovation in AT development and research.

Portability to promote independence describes AT that offers flexibility to be used in various settings and that moves with the user. This is especially important given the requirement for schools to educate students with disabilities in the least restrictive environment. Portable technology enhances opportunities for students with disabilities to engage in educational experiences alongside their peers without disabilities. With more affordable portable technology becoming commercially available, such as specialized software that runs from a jump drive on any computer, more education environments are becoming less restrictive.

Interoperability refers to devices that can be used on multiple platforms, such as a Windows operating system (OS), Mac OS, or any Internet browser. The lack of interoperability can serve as a significant factor to AT abandonment (Bausch, Ault, Emenova, & Behrmann, 2008). Interoperability can also refer more broadly to the design of a system or a device that shares information such as a software program that sends reports to a school's integrated data management system. When students' clinical use of devices or accommodations is synchronized with achievement or assessment data systems, more data will be available to understand the difference AT can make for students.

Conclusion

As the digital generation continues to see technology as integral to their lives, schools are being pushed to better understand ways that these tools can become a part of the teaching and learning experience. A growing number of educators see technology as a way to enhance the educational experience for all students, including those who struggle because the curriculum or materials are not accessible to meet their needs.

Yet research and public rhetoric on technology effectiveness is too often locked in a research paradigm that casts technology as an "intervention" rather than an enabling ecological factor (Zhao, Pugh, Sheldon, & Byers, 2002). The conundrum of innovation outpacing research is described as:

> This lack of hard evidence leads some educators to question the efficacy of incorporating these new technology-based learning experiences, such as those involving digital media and online social networking, and the urgency of investment in what they consider unproven strategies. Conversely, proponents of technology investment reason that digital media are already a prevalent fixture in the lives of contemporary students, so waiting for research to confirm the promise of digital innovation before committing to expanded experimentation is unwise. To proponents, the question is not whether technology should be used in classrooms, but *how* it should be used (Wellings & Levine, 2009, p. 3).

A growing body of evidence indicates that technology *can* enhance teaching and learning to break through the challenges to the vision represented in the NETP. Personalization and connected teaching are keys to breakthrough learning through which educators can enable all students to:

- Reach their academic and social potential
- Engage in tailored learning content and experiences
- Make connections between in and out of school learning, identities, and networks of collaboration and engagement
- Participate and integrate into all aspects of education and society

Each chapter incorporates these concepts as core values and presents a kaleidoscopic view of the role of inclusive technology in assessment, exergaming, professional learning networks, social media, the minds of innovators, and UDL.

References

Artiles, A. J., & Bal, A. (2008). The next generation of disproportionality research: Toward a comparative model in the study of equity in ability differences. *The Journal of Special Education, 42*(1), 4–14.

Bausch, M. E., Ault, M. J., Emenova, A. S., & Behrmann, M. M. (2008). Going beyond AT devices: Are AT services being considered? *Journal of Special Education Technology, 23*(2), 1–16.

Benedict, R. E., & Baumgardner, A. M. (2009). A population approach to understanding children's access to assistive technology. *Disability and Rehabilitation, 31*(7), 582–592.

Bethell, C. D., Read, D., Blumberg, S. J., & Newacheck, P. W. (2008). What is the prevalence of children with special health care needs? Toward an understanding of variations in findings and methods across three national surveys. *Maternal Child Health Journal, 12*, 1–14.

Cataldi, E. F., Laird, J., & KewalRamani, A. (2009). *High school dropout and completion rates in the United States: 2007* (NCES 2009-064). Washington, DC: National Center for Education Statistics, Institute of Education Sciences, U.S. Department of Education. Retrieved from http://nces.ed.gov/pubsearch/pubsinfo.asp?pubid=2009064.

Centers for Disease Control and Prevention (2003). *National survey of children's health*. Retrieved April 5, 2010, from www.cdc.gov/nchs.

Centers for Disease Control and Prevention. (2007, February 9). *Prevalence of Autism spectrum disorders – Autism and developmental disabilities monitoring network, 14 sites, United States, 2002* (Vol. 56/SS-1). Atlanta, GA: U.S. Department of Health and Human Services, Centers for Disease Control and Prevention.

Chandler, M. A. (2009, January 4). More and more, schools got game: Teachers turn to simulations, other software for variety of lessons. *The Washington Post*. Retrieved from http://www.washingtonpost.com.

Christensen, C. M., Horn, M. B., & Johnson, C. W. (2008). *Disrupting class: How disruptive innovation will change the way the world learns*. New York: McGraw Hill.

Cortiella, C. (2009). *The state of learning disabilities*. New York, NY: National Center for Learning Disabilities. Retrieved April 5, 2009, from http://www.LD.org/stateofld.

Fuchs, D., Fuchs, L. S., & Stecker, P. M. (2010). The "blurring" of special education in a new continuum of general education placements and services. *Exceptional Children, 76*(3), 301–323.

García, S. B., & Guerra, P. (2004). Deconstructing deficit thinking: Working with educators to create more equitable learning environments. *Education and Urban Society, 36*(2), 150–168.

Gray, T., Silver-Pacuilla, H., Overton, C., & Brann, A. (2010, January). *Unleashing the power of innovation for assistive technology*. National Center for Technology Innovation. Washington, DC: American Institutes for Research. Retrieved April 2, 2010, from http://www.nationaltechcenter.org/index.php/2009/12/11/rpt-innovation-for-assistive-technology/.

Gray, L., Thomas, N., & Lewis, L. (2010). *Educational technology in U.S. public schools: Fall 2008* (NCES 2010–034). U.S. Department of Education, National Center for Education Statistics. Washington, DC: U.S. Government Printing Office.

Greaves, T., & Hayes, J. (2008). *America's digital schools 2008: The six trends to watch*. Shelton, CT: MDR. Retrieved from http://www.schooldata.com.

Ito, M., Horst, H., Bittanti, M., Boyd, D., Herr-Stephenson, B., Lange, P. G., et al. (2008, November). *Living and learning with new media: Summary of findings from the Digital Youth Project*. Chicago: The John D. and Catherine T. MacArthur Foundation Reports on Digital Media and Learning.

Johnson, L., Smith, R., Levine, A., & Haywood, K. (2010). *2010 Horizon report: K-12 edition*. Austin, TX: The New Media Consortium.

Kapperman, G., Sticken, J., & Heinze, A. (2002). Survey of the use of assistive technology by Illinois students who are visually impaired. *Journal of Visual Impairment and Blindness, 96*(2), 106–108.

Kelly, S. M. (2008). *Correlates of assistive technology use by students who are visually impaired in the U.S.: Multilevel modeling of the special education elementary longitudinal study*. Unpublished doctoral dissertation, Northern Illinois University, Illinois.

Lemke, C., Coughlin, E., & Reifsneider, D. (2009). *Technology in schools: What the research says: An update*. Culver City, CA: Commissioned by Cisco.

Lenhart, A., Arafeh, S., Smith, A., & Macgill, A. R. (2008, April). *Writing, technology and teens*. Washington, DC: Pew Internet & American Life Project and the National Commission on Writing.

Lenhart, A., Ling, R., Campbell, S., & Purcell, K. (2010). *Teens and mobile phones*. Washington, DC: Pew Internet & American Life Project.

Lenhart, A., Madden, M., Rankin-Macgill, A., & Smith, A. (2007). *Teens and social media*. Washington, DC: Pew Internet & American Life Project.

Lyle, E. E. (2010). *A giant leap and a big deal: Delivering on the promise of equal access to broadband to people with disabilities*. FCC Omnibus Broadband Initiative (OBI) Working Reports Series Number 2. Retrieved May 4, 2010, from http://download.broadband.gov/plan/fcc-omnibus-broadband-initiative-(obi)-working-report-giant-leap-big-deal-delivering-promise-of-equal-access-to-broadband-for-people-with-disabilities.pdf.

McCrummen, S. (2010, June 11). Some educators question if whiteboards, other high-tech tools raise achievement. *The Washington Post*. Retrieved from http://www.washingtonpost.com/wp-dyn/content/article/2010/06/10/AR2010061005522.html.

Mulye, T. P., Park, M. J., Nelson, C. D., Adams, S. H., Irwin, C. E., Jr., & Brindis, C. D. (2009). Trends in adolescent and young adult health in the United States. *Journal of Adolescent Health, 45*, 8–24.

National Longitudinal Transition Study – 2. (2005). *Fast facts: High school completion by students with disabilities*. Retrieved May 4, 2010 from http://www.nlts2.org/fact_sheets/nlts2_fact_sheet_2005_11.pdf.

National School Boards Association. (2007). *Creating and connecting: Research and guidelines on online social – and educational – networking*. Retrieved May 6, 2010 from http://www. nsba.org/site/docs/41400/41340.pdf.

Nielsen. (2009). *How teens use media: A Nielsen report on the myths and realities of teen media trends*. New York, NY: The Nielsen Company.

Pew Research Center. (2010). *Millennials: A portrait of generation Next. Confident. Connected. Open to Change*. Washington, DC: Pew Research Center.

Picciano, A. G., & Seaman, J. (2009, January). *K-12 online learning: A 2008 follow-up of the survey of U.S. school district administrators*. The Sloan Consortium. Retrieved March 6, 2009, from http://www.sloanconsortium.org/publications/survey/pdf/k12_online_learning_2008.pdf.

Project Tomorrow. (2010, March). *Creating our future. Speak Up 2009 national findings*. Retrieved April 8, 2010, from http://www.tomorrow.org/speakup/speakup_reports.html.

Quinn, B. S., Berhmann, M., Mastriopieri, M., & Chung, Y. (2009). Who is using assistive technology in schools? *Journal of Special Education Technology, 24*(1), 1–13.

Safran, S. P. (2008). Why youngsters with autistic spectrum disorders remain underrepresented in special education. *Remedial and Special Education, 29*(2), 90–95.

Schnoes, C., Reid, R., Wagner, M., & Marder, C. (2006). ADHD among students receiving special education services: A national survey. *Exceptional Children, 72*(4), 483–496.

Serfass, C., & Peterson, R. L. (2007). A guide to computer-managed IEP record systems. *Teaching Exceptional Children, 40*(1), 16–21.

Shuler, C. (2009). *Pockets of potential: Using mobile technologies to promote children's learning*. New York: The Joan Ganz Cooney Center at Sesame Workshop.

THE Journal. (2008). Retrieved from http://thejournal.com/articles/2008/05/01/together-at-last. aspx?sc_lang=en.

U.S. Department of Education. (2010). *2010 National Educational Technology Plan*. http:www. ed.gov/technology/netp-2010

U.S. Department of Health and Human Services, Health Resources and Services Administration, Maternal and Child Bureau. (2007). *The national survey of children with special health care needs chartbook 2005–2006*. Rockville, MD: U.S. Department of Health and Human Services.

U.S. Federal Communications Commission. (2010). *Connecting America: The national broadband plan*. Retrieved from http://www.broadband.gov/plan.

Van Horn, R. (2007). Educational games. *Phi Delta Kappan, 89*(1), 73–74.

Watson, J., & Gemin, B. (2008). *Using on-line learning for at-risk students and credit recovery*. Vienna, VA: North American Council for Online Learning. Retrieved from http://www.inacol. org/research/promisingpractices/NACOL_CreditRecovery_PromisingPractices.pdf.

Wellings, J., & Levine, M. (2009). The digital promise: Transforming learning with the innovative uses of technology. New York: Joan Ganz Cooney Center at Sesame Workshop.

Zhao, Y., Pugh, K., Sheldon, S., & Byers, J. L. (2002). Conditions for classroom technology innovation. *Teachers College Record, 104*(3), 482–515.

The Power of Social Networking for Professional Development

Elizabeth Bonsignore, Derek Hansen, April Galyardt, Turadg Aleahmad, and Steve Hargadon

Introduction

> ...*something amazing happened. A world began to emerge in which "we" (or people like us) were creators. We could start a blog; we could upload and share photos and videos; we could even build an encyclopedia.*
>
> (Hargadon, 2009, p. 1)

Our foray into the "age of participation" (Grossman, 2006) continues at a staggering pace. In August 2009, Wikipedia hit the three million mark for articles in English (Johnson, 2009). In all, it contains over ten million articles in 250 languages, created and maintained by half a million active contributors (Johnson, 2009). In early 2009, YouTube was the third most active Web site in the world, with ten billion video views per month. In May 2009, Facebook became the top social network worldwide, increasing its membership over 105%, to 112 million visitors, during that year (Curve, 2010). Indeed, social networking sites such as Facebook, LinkedIn, and MySpace are forecast to grow to one billion participants by 2012 (Alexa, 2009). These statistics suggest radical new opportunities for participatory learning with increasingly accessible technologies. Today's low-cost collaborative tools and frameworks, along with near global network connectivity, offer the potential for all people to be active community contributors, with low barriers to entry and worldwide reach. Almost anyone can be a content creator, not just a content consumer (Asare, 2009; Kuntz, 2009).

Despite the booming success of some social networking sites and the public enthusiasm that comes with them, many fail to develop a strong sense of community and are not able to retain members or sustain active participation. Further, not all participants have charitable goals: terrorists and criminals can exploit the power of social media tools. Many educators and parents are concerned by negative outcomes that are often

E. Bonsignore (✉)
University of Maryland, College Park, MD, USA
e-mail: ebonsign@umd.edu

T. Gray and H. Silver-Pacuilla (eds.), *Breakthrough Teaching and Learning:*
How Educational and Assistive Technologies are Driving Innovation,
DOI 10.1007/978-1-4419-7768-7_3, © Springer Science+Business Media, LLC 2011

associated with online environments, such as gossip, wasted time, cyber-bullying, and ruined reputations (Hargadon, 2009). School administrators and the communities they serve have experienced scandals when teachers misuse social media with students (Jackson, 2010). Teachers themselves have been victims of cyber-bullying (Labi, 2010). The volume of publicly available personal data also poses a threat to privacy. Special education teachers in particular are often concerned that their students' privacy will be compromised if they share information about individual education plans (IEPs) with colleagues, even if they are collaborating to improve lesson plans for those students (C. Southard, personal interview, April 3, 2010).

Still, the potential to develop social participation models and personalized learning networks that benefit community members remains high. Enabling informed participation and raising awareness of the potential for misuse can mitigate harmful effects. Zhao and Qiu (this volume) explore the participation patterns and potential benefits of children's use of social media in and out of school.

Innovative educators are in a unique position to be advocates for good, and can use relevant real-world phenomena such as cyber-bullying as teachable moments, for students and colleagues alike. Social media "building blocks" (Hargadon, 2009) or "Web2.0" components,[1] such as threaded discussion forums and chat, can be combined with online learning tools such as webinars to create effective, participatory learning environments. Teachers who use social media technologies to advance their own technical knowledge and professional development will be better able to educate students to use them effectively and ethically.

The variety of collaborative communication tools available within online communities demonstrates the potential merits of developing personalized learning networks, whether we are discussing students or teachers. For many people, however, social networks are limited to social activities related to leisure, not work, and friends and families, not professional colleagues. Educators involved with innovative online communities such as Classroom 2.0 (CR2.0) advocate the term "educational networking" to help avoid potential misconceptions and negative connotations about social networking (Hargadon, 2009).

An underlying theme of the chapters in this book, and emphasized in the National Educational Technology Plan (U.S. Department of Education, 2010), is to promote innovative practices using emerging information and communications technologies to ensure that all students can engage in personalized learning. Personalized learning using innovative technologies can and should be a goal for teachers' professional development as well. Table 1 maps the use of social media for education to both students and teachers. When educators engage in conversations – instead of one-way, one-textbook-fits-all approaches – opportunities abound to personalize the learning that will take place. In effect, education-based social network sites can create their own "differentiated instruction," by teachers, for teachers.

---

[1]We define Web2.0 as both a set of open-source social media tools that support collaboration and a group of people using these tools as they engage in a collaborative community of practice, improving individually even as they participate collectively.

Table 1 Mapping goals for personalized learning to teachers

Inclusive social media as catalysts for personalized learning	
Using social media, educators can effectively support <u>students</u> to....	*Using social media, educators can effectively support <u>each other</u> to....*
...reach their academic and social potential	...reach their personal and professional potential
...engage in tailored learning content and experiences	...engage in professional development content and teaching experiences tailored to their needs, experience, and comfort levels
...make connections between in- and out-of-school learning, identities, and networks of collaboration	...make connections between in-classroom and online teaching opportunities
	...establish networks for professional collaboration
...participate and integrate into all aspects of education and society	...participate and integrate social media components into their teaching practices and professional development
	...enhance their ability to foster their students' critical knowledge and ethical use of social media

As noted by a CR2.0 member who is a leader in special education and assistive technology circles within the CR2.0 community, her local school district, and beyond:

> Every year you're going to need your own personal learning team. Every year, with different kids, you might need someone who has expertise in certain behavioral areas – like autism – or in cognitive issues or content areas. In the network, you have people to connect with who can guide you to the resources you need (C. Southard, personal communication/interview, April 3, 2010).

In keeping with a focus on personalized breakthrough learning, this chapter examines the ways in which participation in social networking sites not only promotes resource sharing among educators, but also contributes to personalized professional development. We provide an in-depth look at one of the most successful grassroots social networking sites for education professionals, CR2.0. We detail some of the factors that led to the success of CR2.0, the activities its members engage in, and the benefits they receive from being part of the community. We pay special attention to members who work in the areas of special education and assistive technologies. In many cases, there may be only one individual who supports the assistive technology or special education needs for a single school or school district. These specialized educators stand to benefit the most from social media technologies and networks particularly in those instances where access to other experts is not available locally.

Collaborative Learning Communities

Social models of learning claim that we learn from our experiences of participating in daily life, and that we develop our identities and professional skills supported by our personal networks of family, friends, and coworkers (Lave & Wenger, 1991). Such social views of learning apply to teachers as well as to their students. Historically, however, professional development programs for teachers have too often focused on one-stop, one-size-fits-all workshops delivered by "experts" in a top-down approach. The techniques presented in these traditional programs have been criticized as procedural, surface-level models that characterize teachers as technicians who use well-defined instructional formulas developed by education researchers (Butler et al., 2004). Ironically, contemporary theories of learning that emphasize continual, socially influenced personal growth have rarely been applied to professional development programs for the teachers who are charged with practicing these theories to nurture their students into becoming lifelong learners (Clarke & Hollingsworth, 2002).

Professional development programs need not be broadcast in one-sided, carefully sequenced seminars. More recently, collaborative inquiry models that emphasize socially constructed knowledge and reflections on best teaching practices have become more prevalent (Butler et al., 2004; Farooq, Schank, Harris, Fusco, & Schlager, 2007). By sharing personal experiences, knowledge, and resources in online communities, every teacher can develop his/her own personal identity as an effective educational practitioner in the company of supportive, like-minded peers and mentors. In some cases, simply hearing or reading about questions or concerns of colleagues who are experiencing similar issues in the classroom can help a teacher learn how he or she might apply the information to his or her situation. People have better memory for information they regard as important to themselves and that is tied to questions they may encounter (Anderson, 2005), making the just-in-time learning of online communities particularly memorable.

Collaborative learning communities offer opportunities to exchange valuable, timely information in relaxed settings, as in the informal chats that occur around an office water cooler or in a teachers' lounge (Fisher, Durrance, & Hinton, 2004). Supported by social media tools in a collaborative learning community, teachers can participate at any level they feel comfortable, observing and engaging as they gain experience. Ultimately, while individual educators focus on improving their own personal teaching and administrative practices, they contribute to the joint enterprise of enhancing educational experiences for all.

What Are Communities of Practice?

Collaborative approaches for professional development help teachers jointly develop best practices for student learning. Teachers get together locally in their schools or externally in meetings outside their districts to improve existing teaching practices or to develop new ones. A "Communities of Practice" (CoP) framework is often used to describe these collaborative programs as well as the informal discussions that occur between classes and over lunch. The CoP concept characterizes learning as an apprentice-like process, in which an individual develops a professional identity within a community while moving through various stages of participation in that community (Lave & Wenger, 1991). For example, in an educational setting, a preservice teacher would work in tandem with experienced educators, iteratively assuming partial roles in the classroom on the way to becoming a full participant in the school. She develops her own personal, professional identity as a teacher as she engages in more central roles. Thus, she learns the "practice" of an educator – not in the sense of practicing the piano, but in the sense of the practice of law or medicine. This process of internalizing a professional practice helps someone *become* a teacher, not just know what a teacher does.

Lave and Wenger (1991) coined the phrase, "legitimate peripheral participation," to describe this process. It is "legitimate," because the professional community accepts that the preservice teacher has the potential to become a certified, in-service educator. The process is "peripheral," because preservice educators initially practice at the edges of active teaching situations, and gradually try out more direct teaching tasks. The process includes "participation," because it is through doing that the novice learns the practice of teaching; the community's knowledge is situated in the practices of its members, not just contained within books and formal institutions.

The members who comprise a CoP are "bound together by shared expertise and a passion for joint enterprise" (Wenger & Snyder, 2000, p. 139). While some CoPs are formally recognized, most develop informally at first, and may not be explicitly recognized at all. The value of a successful educational CoP lies in its ability to support individuals in becoming effective educators, while simultaneously promoting the ongoing self-reflection and refinement of the educational practice itself. Theoretically, a CoP supports both individual and collective learning, and encourages the success of the community and the individual without discounting the needs and contributions of either.

Practically speaking, many collaborative professional development initiatives never evolve into sustained, thriving COPs, especially those whose members are geographically distributed and strapped by time constraints, as is so common. The challenge for professional development programs is to provide multiple, diverse opportunities and formats for their members to connect, communicate, and collaborate, in ways that are meaningful on a personal level as well as an institutional level. Most researchers and proponents of CoPs would agree that a community must develop organically and cannot be forced by design (Barab, MaKinster, & Scheckler, 2003; Koch & Fusco, 2008; Wenger & Snyder, 2000). Still, if we remain aware of some common features of successful communities, effective CoPs for educators can be designed for, or in other words be "cultivated." Before detailing what is known about successful communities, and the tools and infrastructure that support their growth, let us consider what is known about how people participate and interact in online communities.

Participation in Online Communities

Over the past decade, studies of online communities have revealed surprisingly consistent patterns of participation and interaction. These studies have enabled the development of interesting models representing the structural dynamics of communities and offer insights into how people's online behavior evolves over time. Most models categorize online user behavior in terms of levels of familiarity, skill, and active participation with the community or the technology (Preece & Shneiderman, 2009). Typically, there is a relative decrease in the numbers of members who actively participate at each level, creating a funnel effect. For example, Porter (2008) identified four categories of user behavior, with associated participation levels: interested (100%), first-time use (30%), regular use (20%), and passionate use (2%). Through a method known as "social technographics profiling," Li and Bernoff (2008) have conducted large-scale surveys (as many as 10,000 users) to profile similar participation roles.

Bernoff (2010) emphasizes that all participants engage in an online community at some level, but to varying degrees, and that most people participate in multiple, overlapping ways. For example, a "collector" could use RSS feeds, and then serve as a "critic" by posting reviews of services based on her RSS feed summaries. Intuitively, teachers can relate these models of participation to the range of cognitive and sociocultural models of learning. A primary goal for educational communities is to offer multiple avenues for individuals to contribute.

Because people can play multiple roles as they participate in online communities, Bernoff (2010) used a ladder analogy rather than a funnel. Inactive participants and "spectators," sometimes referred to as "lurkers," are situated at the bottom rungs of the ladder, while "creators," individuals who publish blogs or upload multimedia, reside at the top. The ladder analogy provides a useful visual metaphor to characterize participation patterns and percentages; however, it may suggest too strongly that people should be walking up it, rather than traversing it at their own pace and comfort level.

What if we simply turn the ladder on its side? Now we can envision a participatory learning model for online communities that echoes principles from differentiated instruction, in which teachers provide a variety of pedagogical mechanisms to scaffold diverse sets of learners (Tomlinson, 2000). This view offers equal importance to every category of participation. A horizontal framework is also more attractive than a ladder metaphor from a special education perspective. When coupled with the concept of "legitimate peripheral participation," the horizontal framework reflects differentiated instruction and supports principles from Universal Design for Learning, as discussed in Rose's chapter, such as

- Support recognition learning, provide multiple, flexible methods of presentation
- Provide multiple, flexible methods of expression and apprenticeship
- Provide multiple, flexible options for engagement (Hall, Strangman, & Meyer, 2003)

An effective visual model using such a horizontal perspective is the Reader-to-Leader framework (Preece & Shneiderman, 2009). Figure 1 depicts the Reader-to-Leader framework. Note that this graphic, with its arrows running between categories in both directions, makes the individual's movement through various participation states more visible, more representative of the ways in which she/he

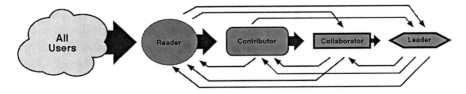

Fig. 1 The Reader-to-Leader framework of technology-mediated social participation (Preece & Shneiderman, 2009)

might engage with social media. While its roles and descriptions may not be as complete as the Li and Bernoff ladder (Bernoff, 2010), the Reader-to-Leader framework provides an equalizing basis to describe how people participate in online communities using social media. The Participation Ladder analogy, which estimates about 70% of people participating in online communities are spectators, places them near "the bottom of the ladder." In contrast, the Reader-to-Leader framework places the spectator, or "reader," on equal footing with all other participation profiles. It is important to recognize that not all benefits of community membership are tied to active participation, as many people benefit considerably from "overhearing the crowd" (Hansen, 2009).

Tools and Infrastructure to Support CoPs

The types of communication tools available and accessible to members affect online participation behaviors. For example, threaded conversation tools such as e-mail lists are ideal for supporting ongoing question and answer discussions, as well as provision of social support. In contrast, wikis are ideal for creating community repositories that aggregate information into reusable content (Hansen, 2007). Other technologies like wall posts, friending, regularly scheduled webinars, chat sessions, and face-to-face meetings all provide unique ways for individuals to interact and build social capital[2] (Resnick, 2002).

Changes to the communication platform can also dramatically affect the social maintenance of a community, defining the ways people can cause social problems (such as "holy wars") as well as potential solutions to those problems (Hansen, 2007). Understanding how specific Web2.0 building blocks such as wikis or discussion forums support different design goals is an important endeavor that is just beginning to be explored by researchers. For example, Ren, Kraut, and Kiesler (2007) discuss which tools are best to apply to "common-bond" communities made up of tight-knit friendship groups versus "common-identity" communities made up of strangers who

---

[2]Social capital refers to the number and types of resources that an individual can access to meet goals or complete tasks, based on the types and strengths of social connections she/he has, e.g., friends and acquaintances (Lin, 2001). Resnick (2002) connected features of social media technologies with the types of social connections and interactions they can promote.

have a common interest. While some technologies support certain activities better, it is important to realize that people can use the same technological infrastructure in amazingly diverse ways as attested by the many flavors of e-mail lists. These studies highlight the importance of allowing community members to choose their own tools for exploring, communicating, and accomplishing their own growth.

Today, open-source, social media have increased opportunities to support personalized, professional development experiences. Web2.0 building blocks that have grown from early online community communications components are detailed in Hargadon (2009) and Wenger, White, and Smith (2009). Examples of these building blocks include community communication and interaction tools such as discussion forums, which enable members to participate in topics of interest over time in a semiconversational flow, or groups, which are subcommunities within the larger networked community that offer a means for existing special interest affiliations to expand, and enable new connections to be created and focused around ad hoc projects, topics, or timely events.

Entities like Ning (http://www.ning.com/) and Grou.ps (http://grou.ps/) allow those without a technical background to "drag and drop" these technology tools into a community site, creating complex highly interactive Web sites in minutes rather than years. Ning, which hosts CR2.0, spawned a host of innovative communities with their easy-to-use interface and feature-rich free plan. When Ning announced in early 2010 that they would no longer support the free plan, educators were distraught and banded together to find free alternatives. Their strong reactions attest to the need for cheap (or free), user-friendly community-building tools for educators and the reliance of many educators on current tools that may or may not be sustainable at those pricing levels.

Classroom 2.0: A Case in Point

CR2.0 started as a "social network for educators interested in the use of Web2.0 in education," as a place to enable educators to see and actually experience "how personally transformative it could be to build or be part of a personal learning network online." (Hargadon, 2009, p. 5). CR2.0 (Fig. 2) numbers among the largest, possibly most popular, and consistently fastest growing groups of educators seeking to integrate read/write Web technologies and twenty-first century literacy activities and resources into their teaching practices. The Ning framework was developed to include many of the collaborative social media tools, or Web2.0 building blocks, by default. The variety of tools offered by Ning allows community moderators and members to customize the ways community members collaborate and learn from each other.

CR2.0 members include teachers (K-16), technologists, students, and researchers sharing their ideas, concerns, blogs, classroom projects, and wikis – globally via their online network, and locally in their individual schools and districts. The diverse CR2.0 community offers insight into the resource sharing and mentoring practices

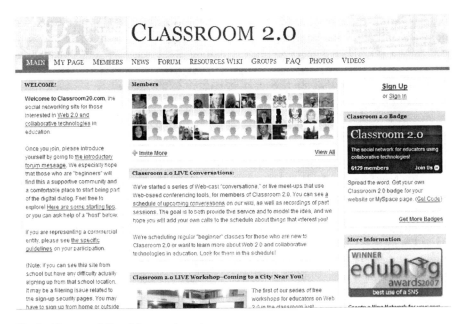

Fig. 2 Classroom2.0 social network, main page

of educators, who are collaborating globally, across geographic boundaries, yet also transferring and applying these experiences locally in their classrooms.

While the overall population composition is a diverse mix of skills and experience, each member joining CR2.0 seems bound by a common core endeavor: to engage with one another in learning how they might harness and use emerging technologies to inspire students, colleagues, friends, and relatives to become lifelong learners. From the beginning, there was a strong desire to have the community model the value of using social media in educational contexts. A more implicit, but not less significant, theme is one of support: teachers who are hesitant about their abilities and desires to use new, collaborative technologies can come here to explore, question, and experiment with like-minded compatriots.

A primary task for experienced members is to ensure that the community remains especially welcoming to beginners. "Participatory learning" is a recurring phrase woven throughout discussions, podcasts, and member blogs, binding together the community themes of innovative teaching and professional development support. Within a few months after the site's launch in the spring of 2007, a member educator interviewed the community founder, Steve Hargadon, and suggested that the site presented a diverse "buffet" of information. Hargadon replied, *"It's not just about eating, it's about cooking, too."*[3]

---

[3]August, 2007, *"ByteSpeed"* podcast by Tim Holt, El Paso, Texas educator and Classroom2.0 member.

Also during this interview, when asked about how and why the virtual forum for the community was started, Hargadon explained that he was inspired by ongoing discussions (online and at conferences) among K-12 teachers and educational speakers about how to start using blogs and related self-publishing tools in the classroom. He sensed that many educators wanted to try the new technologies, but they were concerned about the time investment required to find and learn to use them, and the risks inherent in exposing their ignorance to students. Hargadon felt that for many, the "edublogosphere"[4] was a great medium in which to explore the idea of self-publishing on the Web, as it could serve as an extension of journal-writing that many were using in classes. Blogs take time and effort to develop a following,[5] and many educators trying it for the first time could give up if not supported by encouraging feedback from or dialogue with an empathetic cohort.

Since its inception on March 24th, 2007, the community has experienced phenomenal growth, likely because it filled a unique niche in the educational landscape. On its first anniversary, just over 7,000 people had joined CR2.0. Six months later, in November 2008, this number had doubled (14,200); today (spring 2011), the network boasts over 52,000 members.

Members have always been encouraged to create special interest groups both within and without the community, such as "Digiskills," "Elementary Reading Teachers," "Technology in Special Education (Inclusion Revolution)," "Social Media 101," among others. In the spring of 2011, CR2.0 listed over 600 special interest groups, though participation rates in each are cyclical and not analyzed in detail for this chapter. The number of special interest groups available to CR2.0 members underscores the value of allowing proactive users to become organizers themselves. In addition to the opportunities to interact via individual and group forums, the site architecture enables fairly easy sharing of embedded technologies such as podcast links, videos, and images/photos. In fact, most of the well-known Web2.0 building blocks are supported by the CR2.0 community infrastructure.

These design features not only enhance the level of engagement a member can have with his community, they also afford development and tracking of member-to-community interactions using social network analysis (Hansen et al., 2010). These techniques reveal underlying community structures, such as level of connectedness (e.g., Barbara has 12 friends; Bill has 250; Claire belongs to 6 groups; Luke is a member of one); or level of participation (e.g., Jim started two discussion threads over the past 6 months, but is active in daily discussions he did not start). These metrics can also uncover connections between members who may not belong to the same groups, but respond to each others' discussion threads (Getoor & Diehl, 2005). Initial results from such social network analysis techniques can then be used to direct more focused study.

---

[4]Bloggers/blogging within the general education and educational technology community.

[5]Steve recalled at the time that those who were encouraging edublogging suggested that it would take an estimated 9 months of effort before a steady "following" or feedback would result from an education-based blog.

CR2.0: Anatomy of an Online Community

Our CR2.0 analysis aimed to characterize a successful educational CoP and the tools that help make it a successful, and outline its potential to promote personalized professional development, particularly in the arena of special education and assistive technology. This requires a focus on both the technologies and social practices that support meaningful engagement around professional development, recognizing their close coupling with one another. Thus, we focus on specific technologies (e.g., forums and wall posts) and the interactions they support; the reasons special education teachers or assistive technologists become members of online communities and their perceived benefits; and some of the challenges of running an online community of practice.

We applied a variety of research methods to meet these goals. Qualitative methods include interviews of key community members, content analysis of discussion forum posts about special education and assistive technology, and insights gained from Steve Hargadon. We use quantitative methods to find patterns in the wealth of data left behind by participants in their everyday interactions with CR2.0. For example, textual analysis of content on profile pages and discussion forum posts helps us understand who participates in the site and what they discuss. Social network analysis enables us to map relationships between people, identify important individuals, and characterize subgroups such as those involved with special education and assistive technology (Hansen, Shneiderman, & Smith, 2010).

Our primary dataset is based on participation patterns and member interaction from March 2007, when the community was first established, through November 2008, our initial data collection date. As such, it gives a picture of the CR2.0 community during its first 20 months of rapid growth and development as a vibrant community of educators. Member profiles and public interactions were downloaded and processed using software developed by one of this chapter's authors (Aleahmad, 2008). We have augmented the primary data set with qualitative analysis of more recent interactions on the CR2.0 site as well as related online communities and social media specific to special education and assistive technology members (e.g., www.assistivetech.ning.com).

In the analysis laid out in the following sections, we examine:

* General membership composition that can be seen from member profiles.
* Participation patterns that are openly observable in CR2.0.
* Joining patterns that reveal the global reach of individuals' networks.
* Discussion styles and patterns and the functions they serve.
* What CR2.0 and communities like it can offer special education professionals.

Community Composition

The primary data analyzed for this chapter consist of CR2.0 member profiles and publicly available online interactions from March 2007 to November 2008, at which time the community boasted over 14,200 members. A more detailed analysis of available member profiles and content for the community's interactions can be found in Galyardt, Aleahmad, Fienberg, Junker, and Hargadon (2009). The data collection process and analysis were coordinated by Steve Hargadon, publicized to the community, and discussed in two online forums (October 2008 and April 2009).[6]

In November 2008, about 2,000 (14%) of the registered members had taken no overt actions in the community beyond creating their profile. At face value, this percentage is on par with estimates of "Inactives," from Li and Bernoff's Participation Ladder (Bernoff, 2010) and other studies of social networks (Golbeck, 2007). However, because the CR2.0 site content is publicly available, there can be a large percentage of people who follow the community discussions but never register. The statistics in Table 2, showing the total number of unique visitors to the site (whether registered member or not), demonstrate the value of CR2.0 content and interactions extend well beyond its membership bounds.

CR2.0 members create a user profile when they join the community. Each user can choose to share personal information such as geographic location (e.g., Sacramento, California), workplace/affiliation (e.g., Smith Middle School), a short biography "About Me," gender, and age/birthday. Some members may elect not to make any of this information public, so there were many gaps in membership profiles. Comprehensive community-wide statistics based on geographic backgrounds (or hometowns) for members was not possible via profile data alone, as only about half of the 14,000 members in our data reported their country. For those who provided explicit information in their profiles, we found CR2.0 membership from 2007 to 2008 represented 115 distinct countries. The majority of members come from English-speaking countries: USA, Australia, UK, Canada, and India. About half the members are Americans, and some of the most active members are Australian.

A significant majority of the members appear to be teachers. Seventy-two percent of profiles contain a variation of the word teacher under About Me: *teach,*

Table 2 Overall visitor numbers compared to registered CR2.0 members

March 2007–May 2010	March 2007–November 2008 (primary data collection timeframe)
1,737,555 Unique visitors made *2,430,764* visits	*390,446* Unique visitors made *587,453* visits
43,281 Registered members	*14,200* Registered members

---

[6]Meeting recording, October 2008: https://sas.elluminate.com/p.jnlp?psid=2008-10-20.1718.M.E2778A53C1F6D563E74CF199BAC39A.vcr; Meeting recording, April 2009: https://sas.elluminate.com/p.jnlp?psid=2008-10-20.1718.M.E2778A53C1F6D563E74CF199BAC39A.vcr.

teacher, teaching. The proportion of teachers may be much higher than observed because of missing data; however, context is missing. For example, we do not know whether the word *teacher* was used in the past, present, or future tense: "I *was* a teacher," "I *am* a teacher," or "I'll *teach when* I graduate."

Just over 10% of all profiles contain the words *college* or *university* under the Affiliation heading. However, it is unclear whether these members are professors, graduate students, undergrads, or even what their disciplinary specialties are. Inspection of individual profiles indicates that some of those affiliated with universities are teachers who have gone to graduate school for master's degrees in education; others are graduate students and professors in computer science who work on education technologies. The only way to ascertain the numbers of members who truly fall within these categories would be to undertake a hand-inspection of the 14,000 profiles.

Multiple Avenues for Participation

"It's kind of like Ellis Island, in an ideal sense. This is an entry point to a new culture." – CR2.0 early member, Discussion post in April 2007 (Member is still active as of April 2010)

The CR2.0 community engages in its practice of socially constructed learning not only in the virtual world – toward the end of its first year, it instituted a plan to hold "face-to-face" workshops as well. Here, those who sport the common "Classroom2.0" badge online can connect with like-minded people around a physical table. The first such conference was held in mid-February 2008. Postconference summaries reflected that it successfully enabled a robust online community to continue to extend its stories of education and technology integration into "the real world." Similarly, Cummings et al. (2002) found that the members of a health discussion group who had experienced both online and offline interactions felt more support and satisfaction with their communities overall. CR2.0 has provided multiple avenues for members to participate in physical spaces since February 2008.

The CR2.0 workshops have always been focused on the beginner and advertise their intent to be hands-on and "much like the Web itself: free, open, engaging, participative, and highly collaborative … if you are a beginner, you are the reason we are holding these workshops!" (Hargadon, n.d.). Regional and national CR2.0 workshops were held almost bimonthly from February 2008 to October 2009, and continue to be scheduled, but on a more infrequent basis.

The workshops are not the only physical forum in which CR2.0 members can gather. Multiple opportunities to meet face-to-face are publicized to the CR2.0 community, to include the large annual *EduBloggerCon* "Social Media in Education

Unconference," and smaller self-organized meetings at a variety of educational technology conferences. During *EduBloggerCon*, participants post discussion topics to a wiki and have opportunities to present ideas to their colleagues in informal, collegial settings. Since 2006, during their annual community conference, the International Society for Technology in Education (ISTE) has supported a "Bloggers' Café," or physical space for interested educators to gather, plug in, and meet individuals they may know in a virtual sense, but have yet to meet face-to-face. The *FutureofEducation. com* live and interactive interview series is also an outgrowth of CR2.0. In effect, the "Beginner Workshops," *EduBloggercon*, the Bloggers' Café, and the Unplugged sessions are yet other means by which the CR2.0 community offers parallel tracks for people at different places in the spectrum of professional development, enabling them to participate at their own levels of experience and comfort.

Community Connections and Joining Patterns

We plotted the location of CR2.0 members in Google Earth (2009) and then drew the connections between them from the wall comments and the forums.[7] By combining the dates that members joined the community with their advertized locations using the Google Earth animation, we were able to observe bursts in new members joining the network. When we look at the animated version of the Google map, we can watch several people join in one town, then a few more from the same town, and then a few more. This behavior pattern, which is repeated across the country and all over the world, suggests that the network is growing through word of mouth.

Many members joined in groups, for example, 4 people from Manhattan, Kansas joined together; later, 7 from Springfield, Massachusetts, and 21 elementary teachers from Wanamingo, Minnesota joined within minutes of each other. We even see one instance in which a block of 50 teachers from all over Pennsylvania joined the network in a space of 10 min. Members are joining with friends from the same school, and they are joining with colleagues at workshops or conferences. This behavioral trend supports research indicating that people are more likely to join a community if their friends are joining it (Backstrom et al., 2009).

In addition, we observed that some cities occur more frequently as member hometowns than we might expect given the size of the cities: Manhattan, Kansas; Greensboro, North Carolina; Salina, Kansas; Colorado Springs, Colorado; Eugene, Oregon. These places are all home to large state universities with large teacher preparation programs. This corresponds with our observation that just over 10% of profiles specify affiliations to universities and colleges.

Members appear to be joining the online community with friends and colleagues they already know. Yet evidence suggests that once the educators have joined the

---

[7]The Google Earth file is available at: http://turadg.aleahmad.net/projects/understanding-classroom-20/.

community, they are using the network to connect with people geographically distant from themselves. Most connections are thousands of miles apart (San Francisco to Topeka), and a large portion are as far as the distance from New York to Melbourne, Australia. This pattern is also evident in the Google Earth dynamic visualization; very few connections between people in the same state are visible. So even though the community appears to be spreading through people who know each other face-to-face, members are using the online tools to reach out to new people who may be able to provide them with information that is not locally available.

Community Discussion Styles

The different features of the site do appear to promote different activities. Forum discussion boards are set up so that replies are made to a topic, while wall comments are made to a person. Members who joined to learn more about specific educational topics may be drawn to the forums, while members who joined for professional camaraderie may find the wall network more inviting. Wall comments seem to support common-bond interactions (identifying with people), whereas forums encourage common-identity interactions (identifying with the community) (Ren et al., 2007). For CR2.0 as a whole, the networks resulting from wall comments versus discussion forums appear to have a small amount of overlap in participants, and the content differs greatly.

In specific cases, however, there can be nuanced interactions between the two communication mechanisms. For example, the "Introductions" discussion thread encourages newcomers to present short bios and backgrounds, which sometimes elicits wall comments in addition to replies within the discussion group. CR2.0 "hosts," or members who volunteer to help newcomers feel at home may communicate in ways that overlap characteristically distinct forum discussion and wall comment groups. Further, a few members are using their wall comment areas in innovative ways. One assistive technologist has used his wall to post short summaries of and links to his "AT Tipscast" podcasting series.

Substantive discussions are much more prominent in the forum area of CR2.0, while the wall comments feature personal introductions and a wide variety of "on-topic" spam.[8] The forums also encouraged denser networks, where discussion flows between all the members of the network. This behavior is in contrast to wall comments, where people may be very active and connect with many individuals, but their friends do not talk to each other. In the wall comments, conversations often take place between pairs of people; in the forums, conversations take place between groups of people.

---

[8]Examples of "on-topic" spam includes automated posts on individual walls across the entire community, requesting votes for grant programs, evaluators for new software programs, and the like.

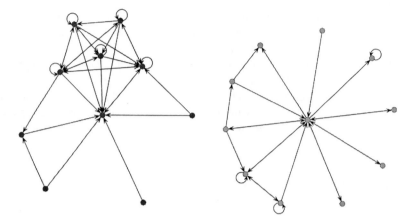

Fig. 3 An ego-network shows a single individual, all of the individuals connected directly to the individual, and all of the connections between these individuals

One way to observe this pattern is through ego-networks. An ego-network is a visualization of network structure that focuses on individuals and the people to whom they are directly connected.

In communities that are discussion-based, ego-networks are often fully connected; all of the individual's friends are friends with each other. In other communities, we observe that some individuals are hubs that connect with many other individuals, but their friends are not directly connected to each other (Adamic, Zhang, Bakshy, and Ackerman, 2008). Ego-networks characteristic of the forums and wall comments are shown in Fig. 3. The patterns observed in the forums are typical discussion community patterns where everyone talks to everyone else. The wall comments are dominated by star-shaped ego-networks where one individual is the center of their local network and their friends are not connected to each other. As a person-to-person interaction medium, the wall comments effectively support introductions and the formation of colleague relationships, or extensions of a member's personal network. A detailed analysis of the CR2.0 textual content is provided in Galyardt et al. (2009).

Connections Specific to Special Education Teachers

Approximately 100 members in our data who identified themselves as special education teachers or assistive technologists were also active in discussions and posting comments on their colleagues' and their own comment walls. This is a small niche group, under 2% of the total population, although it is typical of other niche groups within the larger community. Members were identified based on their membership in special interest groups associated with special education (e.g., "Technology in Special Education/Inclusion Revolution") or by describing themselves using

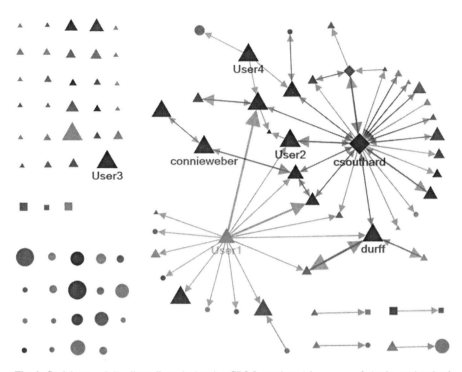

Fig. 4 Social network "wall post" graph showing CR2.0 members (*shown as nodes*) who are involved with special education or assistive technologies. A line (i.e., edge) indicates that one person posted on the wall of another person (*the recipient of the arrow*). *Thicker lines* indicate multiple posts. Larger nodes posted more messages to the community forums and darker nodes have received wall posts from many CR2.0 members. Isolate nodes with no connections (*on the left*) have not received or provided any wall posts to other members of this subgroup. The shape of the nodes indicates group membership: *triangles* indicates Technology in Special Education, *square* indicates Assistive Technology, *diamonds* indicate membership in both those groups, *circle* nodes belong to no group (just profile mentions)

special education terms in their personal profile. The community interactions of these members were analyzed using social network analysis techniques. Based on these results, a more detailed, qualitative, and largely manual analysis of specific members and their interactions was extended to data presented on the online community site (up to spring, 2010).

The structural pattern of participation shown in Fig. 4 is typical of online community interaction, with a few well-connected members who act as the glue that ties others together, and many others who are isolated or on the periphery of the network. This emphasizes the important role that a handful of people like *csouthard* (whose interview comments are explored in more detail below) and *durff* play within this subcommunity on Ning. From November 2007 to late 2008, *csouthard* posted on 58 other people's wall (21 of whom are "assistive technology" people). It is worth noting that *csouthard* not only posts to others' walls, but she also receives replies from nearly everyone she posts to, suggesting strong reciprocity. In contrast, *User1* posts on many other members' walls but does not receive posts on her own wall.

The sparse nature of this network (i.e., the fact that there are so many isolates) suggests that there could be a greater initiative to welcome others into the group by posting on their walls. The majority of thin lines suggest that relatively few exchanges occur on wall posts in this subgroup, likely because most discussions occur in the forums. Further, the structural pattern reflected in Fig. 4 supports the observation that the ego-networks for wall comments are star-shaped (Fig. 3), as it reveals two to three star-shaped ego-networks that happen to be bridged by the handful of active posters in the "Technology in Special Education" group.

Figure 4 is not a dense network, but seems slightly more connected than the single ego-network graph from Fig. 3 because the active posters shown are from the same special interest group. All the members to whom they are posting are often not connected to anyone but the poster (ego). For example, the members whose walls *csouthard* and *User1* comment on are not connected to one other. A final observation is that many of the active wall posting participants are active in the discussion forums as well, as indicated by their large size (frequent posts). Their dark color indicates that they receive many posts on their wall from members throughout the CR2.0 community.

The "reply graph" in Fig. 5 shows the implicit connections between people based on who replied to whom in the discussion forums. In contrast to the wall post

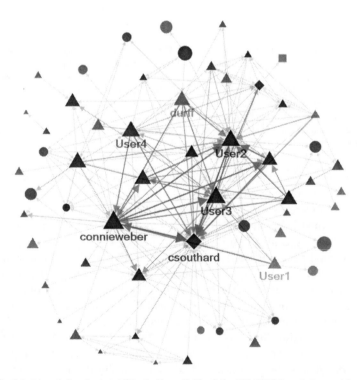

Fig. 5 Social network "reply graph" including all 59 of the 100 CR2.0 assistive tech/specialized members who participated in the discussion threads. A line suggests that one person (*the source*) replied to another person (*the recipient of the arrow*) in a forum

network (Fig. 4), this network is much denser, indicating more inter-related connections and group conversations. This supports the claim that forums are good for building communities, while wall posts are good for making one-on-one connections.

The high density of the graph in Fig. 5 suggests that CR2.0 members involved with special education and assistive technology are fairly well connected to each other, i.e., they may not post to each other's walls often, but they seem to interact with one another in the forums. This is interesting, because many school districts employ only one or two special education teachers to be responsible for an entire school or even district. Locally, they tend to be very isolated. In particular, nearly all of the core members in the center and many of the peripheral members are members of the Technology in Special Education group (they are triangles), showing that the group-specific forums play prominently and help people with a similar interest come together.

How Do Key CR2.0 Members Use Social Media?

Overall, educators are using online communities like CR2.0 to connect with experts and marshal resources that are not available to them locally. They are adding their personal voices and concerns to the broad discussion pool and considering the questions of others. What benefits and challenges do key individuals in special education see arising from these opportunities for personalized professional development? How do they use social media to develop personal learning networks and improve their practice?

Our network analysis of the "nodes" (members) of the CR2.0 community highlighted a few members who were most active in welcoming special education teachers and assistive technologists and encouraging increased levels of participation. We conducted interviews with two CR2.0 members from this group. Both are active bloggers, tweeters, and members of another online Ning community focused on assistive technologists, AssistiveTech, (http://assistivetech.ning.com). Our goal was to get their perspectives on the opportunities and challenges that social media tools and networks offer for special education teachers and assistive technologists.

One interviewee, Christine Southard, is an elementary school inclusion teacher, dual certified in elementary and special education, and based in New York. The inclusion classroom in which she works follows the co-teaching model. As such, she teaches alongside a general education teacher, acting as the special education or inclusion teacher. Her experiences provide insight into the potential benefits and associated challenges that teachers face when learning to navigate social networks and use social media in inclusion classrooms.

The second interviewee, Brian Wojcik, is an assistive technologist and coordinator of the Illinois State University Special Education Assistive Technology (SEAT) Center. He helps preservice and practicing education professionals to develop skills related to using assistive technology in the classroom. Just as Southard collaborates daily with a general education teacher, Wojcik also collaborates with educational technologists and Information Technology (IT) specialists from general education.

Together, the personal reflections of Southard and Wojcik provide us with complementary perspectives of the special education teacher and a technologist who works closely with them to help children realize their own personal learning goals.

The experiences of Christine Southard offer us a case study of a K-12 teacher who has evolved from reader to leader (Fig. 2) in her personal professional development over the past 3 years. During this time, she has grown from engaged-spectator to group creator, cheerleader, and community-wide conversationalist. Today, in addition to shepherding the "*Inclusion Revolution: Technology in Special Education*" special interest group, she founded in CR2.0 during the summer of 2007, she blogs, tweets, presents at conferences at the local and national level, and is a member-at-large in the ISTE Special Education Technologies Special Interest Group (SETSIG). In her view, social media offer a means to engage in a dialogue on topics of professional and personal interest:

> Magazines are a form of professional development, but they are one-sided in the sense that I can read them, and I can think about them, but that's it. However, if you are on a network, then the information in that article becomes multi-faceted. You can link out to it, comment about it with others within the discussion space, you can see or share related links or blogs or other discussions. You can request that a community like CR2.0 invite the author or other experts on that topic to speak about it online. Social networking takes your learning to new levels.
>
> (C. Southard, personal interview, April 3, 2010)

Southard's emphasis here is on the ways in which content can be connected and enriched through interactions by many individuals in a community. Multifaceted connections need not be limited to content, however. Both Wojcik and Southard agree that a primary strength of online communities is their inherent ability to connect people in ways that were not possible before social media technologies were widely and openly available.

They stressed that special education teachers and assistive technologists work under especially isolated conditions. For this very reason, they argue, it is imperative that individuals involved in special education and assistive technologies find a social media tool or platform in which they can easily make connections with others like them. In their own words:

> There is a high-burnout rate when it comes to keeping teachers in special education classrooms. Special education teachers often don't really have anyone to turn to in their school district. Most don't have anyone locally, because their position and caseload may be so unique. Special education, as a discipline, is so broad and diverse it's hard to narrow down. It's important for these teachers to have a network.
>
> (C. Southard, personal interview, April 3, 2010)

> In assistive technology, people tend to practice in isolation. They tend to be one – maybe the only – person within their school system who does assistive technology as a major role, and so a social network or online community becomes a point in which they can connect.

Participating, coming to a social network is going to allow them to connect with others, to share stories, and broaden their understanding of their area of practice.

(B. Wojcik, personal interview, May 3, 2010)

One feature of online communities that Southard and Wojcik find especially important for special education teachers and assistive technologists is the ability for any member to create their own special interest group. Since Southard launched the "Inclusion Revolution Group" in the summer of 2007, its 154 members have shared perspectives and resources on 29 topics of interest to special education teachers and the assistive technologists who work with them. Some topics contain only one post, others between 13 and 20. On average, the group's archived and continuing discussions present a resource for a special education teacher that contains about one topic per month over a period of 3 years. Each thread contains at least one link to another online special education resource, enabling connections to many more special-education-focused resources.

In his role as moderator and facilitator for the *AssistiveTech Ning*, Wojcik has also seen several active groups initiated by individual members. The content of these discussions is open to anyone, but it is also partitioned in a community space that makes it easily accessible and shareable with any individual interested in these "niche" topics. Two groups in the *AssistiveTech Ning* highlight the effectiveness of subgroups within a larger community. One member, a speech language pathologist, has been involved in helping design a communication system that is based on the iPod Touch, for people who have difficulty in communicating with typically verbal communication. One of the first groups to sprout from the *Assistive Tech* community, it was easily created because one member was interested in having a very focused discussion on the connection between literacy and the use of Augmented and Alternative Communication technologies.

Both interviewees would like to see participation levels increase. They emphasize that educators should focus on tailoring their use of social media tools to fit their personal needs and interaction styles.

Designing, Managing, and Participating in Online Communities

Throughout this chapter, we have analyzed CR2.0 social media tools, general member interactions, activities, and attitudes specific to members involved with special education and assistive technology. Our findings highlight various technical affordances that social frameworks provide to communities like CR2.0, in terms of their value to each member individually as well as to the community as a whole. In many ways, features that enable individual customization and personalized participation are the very components that sustain the community itself. Still, challenges remain to ensure that each individual seeking to join the community can find the types of support and opportunities to participate they need, at the times that can help them most. In particular, members involved in special education and assistive technologies face challenges in using social technologies to support the diverse abilities of their students. Their challenges, in turn, raise issues and challenges for community creators, designers, and moderators that can and should be addressed. The following sections summarize both the affordances and challenges for educators who aspire to develop personal learning networks using social media and participating as members of communities like CR2.0.

Affordances to Support Personalized, Participatory Learning

The tools and interfaces (Web2.0 building blocks) that exist in online community infrastructures like CR2.0 provide many professional development opportunities for educators, regardless of specialization.

Social Media Offer Multiple Ways for Members to Personalize Their Interactions

Wall posts and discussion forums enable distinct forms of interaction that support different types of members. Whether you come to CR2.0 to find and connect with a specific colleague or to learn about a specific technology or classroom practice, CR2.0 and online communities like it contain a variety of tools to help you make those connections. Regardless of whether you choose to interact primarily through wall comments, within discussion forums, or a bit of both, you are free to participate in ways that suit your needs.

These public interaction spaces are not the only ways in which educators can participate. According to Brian Wojcik, many assistive technologists and special education teachers will notice a topic of interest, or peruse a profile of someone with whom they identify, and then send them a more traditional, more "secure," direct message. Anecdotal evidence reflects that this is where many members may go to extend and cement their personal learning networks.

Social Media Can Offer Opportunities for Members to Create Their Own Special Interest Groups

Given the power to create their own special interest groups, participants can focus on issues of direct concern to them, and personalize their interaction with the community as a whole. CR2.0 grants its members an easy way to create their own groups and invite like-minded individuals to participate in shared explorations of specialized areas of interest. Groups offer proactive members the power to thrive in the roles of organizer and creator, while simultaneously helping the community grow stronger. CR2.0 encouraged its members to create other Ning networks as well, promoting a sense of openness and a view of educational networking as nonproprietary and noncompetitive. These niche groups and discussions are especially important to individuals involved in special education and assistive technology.

Social Media Offers Opportunities for Members from Diverse Backgrounds to See New Perspectives

Special education teachers and assistive technologists can benefit not only by forming special interest subgroups within the community that enable them to connect and build their personal learning networks. They can also benefit from participating in, or reading about, technologies and tools from general education members or instructional and media technologists.

Both Southard and Wojcik believe their collaboration with general education teachers and IT specialists expanded their ways of thinking about integrating technology into education. For isolated special education teachers and assistive technologists, opportunities to connect with educators who possess different types and levels of expertise are important.

With Social Media, Almost Any Topic of Interest Is Game

Our content analysis of discussion forum threads, whether statistically and qualitatively coded, revealed that CR2.0 members are able to explore a broad spectrum of pedagogical and technical resources. They ask for specific help to improve their teaching practices and their students' learning opportunities. Their discussions and questions run the gamut. They seek practical examples to support their local classroom teaching, such as lesson plans and tips.

They also seek recommendations on developing policies and procedures to support the use of various social media technologies in their school districts and individual schools. They offer opportunities to collaborate with other teachers and classrooms on specific projects, such as podcasting history topics, music, or language learning.

Social Media and Online Communities Offer Isolated Specialists with a Means to Connect with Others Who Might Be Experiencing the Same Challenges or Questions

The special education teacher is fairly isolated – often a population of one in a school or entire school district. It is beneficial for such isolated professionals to use social media to build a personal support network from which to gather ideas and support when needed.

Challenges to Participation and Personalization

Challenges also exist for community builders and moderators. Paying attention to the challenges and identifying some strategies to mitigate their effects on participation is important to ensure all community members can succeed in personalizing their learning and deepening their professional development efforts.

The Rapid Growth of CR2.0 Can Be a Double-Edged Sword

Some newcomers may be overwhelmed with the number of topics and expertise available. New members may find that they do not get responses back to queries or initial posts when the network is large. The ability of any member to join or create a special interest group proved to be a major strategy to deal with the rapid growth and diversity of participants within CR2.0.

Allow for Multiple, Parallel Points of Entry to Include a Wider Group of Educators and Enable More Opportunities for Personalization

Many experienced educators remain comfortable in a "broadcast" communication medium like listserv, and are just beginning to see the benefits of participating in threaded discussions and special interest groups. Many educators are used to evaluating students on their written work, and are hesitant to write something that "will live forever online," in case they were to make a mistake. Keep in mind that there are issues with degree of public identity; issues in terms of confidentiality for students; for comfort with technology in general. Allow them to keep their existing networks, and provide communications tools that enable them to transition as their comfort levels dictate. For example, maintain the direct mail feature and other forms of privacy controls while promoting the CR2.0 workshops and mentoring support mechanisms.

"No More Free Ning!" What Happens When Freely Available Community Infrastructures Become Fee-Based, with Limited Toolsets?

After Ning announced that they would be transitioning their free services to completely fee-based in April 2010, many CR2.0 members reacted passionately. Several discussion threads popped up during the months of April–May 2010 asking questions about where to move, whether to fight, and concerns about what would happen to the archived content, a valuable, searchable reference for professional development and classroom ideas.

The overall sentiment of the comments and online community meetings was *"we are going to rebuild this, no matter what."* Two messages in particular from the ongoing discussions reflect this:

- The hosting platform is no longer the novel or central piece. Social media transcends the individual companies that might provide the service. The community itself, and the tools and interactions that sustain it will carry on, regardless of what platform supports it. However, there can be significant switching costs when changing platforms, particularly if you want to take your prior archived conversations and relationships with you.
- Online communities see social networking as a set of skills versus a platform. Social networking is a group of people coming together and building a body of content that is seen as open and public. The CR2.0 forums, archived webinars, wikis, and wall comments are seen as a repository of information created by the public for the public. The main concern is not whether the community and inter-actions will live on, but how to preserve the content and its accessibility.

Conclusion

CR2.0 may be one of the best examples of an educational community that was founded on, and grew exponentially from, a "natural architecture of participation" (O'Reilly, 2005, p. 3). It was created as a means for a small community of edublog-gers to connect in a common space, where individual content and comments could be aggregated, digested, shared, and disseminated collectively. In less than 4 years, CR2.0 grew from a community of a few hundred early adopters to an educator network of over 50,000 registered members, and untold others who may benefit but never register. We have found that members may join as individuals or in groups, but each person seeks ways to improve personal practice, professional development connections, and understandings about emerging technologies in educational con-texts. We have seen that educators who work in the oft-isolated realm of special education and assistive technologies stand to benefit greatly from connecting with colleagues facing issues and experiences very close to their own, despite any dis-tances in geography or skill level.

Most CR2.0 members do not seem to remain persistently active in community activities over time. However, many have used it as a place to start, as a place to set up a special interest group and perhaps branch off into their own Ning or online community. All networking activities and learning do not take place on CR2.0, but it has opened the conversation to many more individuals who saw the possibilities and were empowered through social media tools and personal desire to join, connect, participate in multiple forums (online and face-to-face), and even strike out on their own. In short, *"CR2.0 may not be the hub, but it's the grease"* (S. Hargadon, personal interview, May 21, 2010).

Overall, CR2.0 and the social media tools embedded in its online framework have enabled educators to develop their own personal learning networks and support the success of their CoP. As noted at the beginning of this chapter, CR2.0 offers a personal professional development model for teachers, one that parallels the personal learning principles that we advocate for students.

References

Adamic, L. A., Zhang, J., Bakshy, E., & Ackerman, M. S. (2008). *Knowledge sharing and yahoo answers: Everyone knows something.* In *WWW '08: Proceeding of the 17th international conference on World Wide Web* (pp. 665–674). New York, NY, USA: ACM.

Aleahmad, T. (2008). *Ning tools* [Computer software], http://github.com/turadg/ning-tools.

Alexa: The Web Information Company (2009), Retrieved February 15, 2009 from http://www.alexa.com.

Anderson, J. R. (2005). Cognitive Psychology and Its Implications: Sixth Edition. New York: Worth Publishing.

Asare, K. (2009). *The federal perspective on technology and innovation.* Keynote address presented at the National Center for Technology Innovation 2009 Innovators' Conference, Washington, D.C. Retrieved from <http://www.nationaltechcenter.org/index.php/2009/09/01/conf09-conference-agenda/>.

Barab, S. A., MaKinster, J. G., & Scheckler, R. (2003). Designing system dualities: Characterizing a web-supported professional development community. *Information Society, 19*(3), 237.

Backstrom, L., Huttenlocher, D., Kleinberg, J., & Lan, X. (2006, August). Group formation in large social networks: Membership, growth, and evolution. In *Proceedings of the 12th ACM SIGKDD International Conference on Knowledge Discovery and Data Mining.* ACM Press: Philadelphia, PA, USA.

Bernoff, J. (2010, January 19). Groundswell: Winning in a world transformed by social technologies. *Social Technographics: Conversationalists get onto the ladder.* Forrester Research industry blog. Retrieved from http://forrester.typepad.com/groundswell/2010/01/conversationalists-get-onto-the-ladder.html.

Butler, D. L., Lauscher, H. N., Jarvis-Selinger, S., & Beckingham, B. (2004). Collaboration and self-regulation in teachers' professional development. *Teaching and Teacher Education, 20*(5), 435–455.

Clarke, D., & Hollingsworth, H. (2002). Elaborating a model of teacher professional growth. *Teaching and Teacher Education, 18*(8), 947–967.

Cummings, J. N., Sproull, L., & Kiesler, S. B. (2002). Beyond hearing: Where the real-world and online support meet. *Group Dynamics: Theory, Research, and Practice, 6*(1), 78-88.

Curve, H. (2010). ComScore: 2009 social networking stats. *ComputerWorld, 15*(12). Retrieved February 10, 2010 from http://news.idg.no/cw/art.cfm?id=B8790C25-1A64-6A71-CEDC88EAA45BCE6F.

Farooq, U., Schank, P., Harris, A., Fusco, J., & Schlager, M. (2007). Sustaining a community computing infrastructure for online teacher professional development: A case study of designing Tapped In. *Computer Supported Cooperative Work, 16*(4–5), 397–429.

Fisher, K. E., Durrance, J. C., & Hinton, M. B. (2004). Information grounds and the use of need-based services by immigrants in Queens, New York: A context-based, outcome evaluation approach. *Journal of the American Society for Information Science & Technology, 55*(8), 754–766.

Galyardt, A., Aleahmad, T., Fienberg, S., Junker, B., & Hargadon, S. (2009). *Analysis of a Web-based network of educators.* Carnegie Mellon University. Retrieved from http://www.stat.cmu.edu/tr/tr878/tr878.pdf.

Google Inc. (2009). Google Earth (Version 5.1) [Software]. Available from http://www.google. com/earth/index.html.

Getoor, L., & Diehl, C. P. (2005). Link mining: a survey. *SIGKDD Explorations Newsletter, 7*(2), 3–12.

Golbeck, J. (2007). The dynamics of web-based social networks: membership, relationships, and change. First Monday, 12(11), Retrieved from http://firstmonday.org/htbin/cgiwrap/bin/ojs/ index.php/fm/article/view/2023/1889.

Grossman, L. (2006). Time person of the year: you. *Time, 168*(26), 38–41.

Hall, T., Strangman, N., & Meyer, A. (2003). *Differentiated instruction and implications for UDL implementation.* Wakefield, MA: National Center on Accessing the General Curriculum (CAST/ NCAC). Retrieved from http://www.cast.org/publications/ncac/ncac_diffinstructudl.html

Hansen, D. L. (2007). Knowledge sharing, maintenance, and use in online support communities. Doctoral Thesis. Ann Arbor: University of Michigan

Hansen, D. L. (2009). Overhearing the crowd: an empirical examination of conversation reuse in a technical support community. In *Proceedings of the fourth international conference on Communities and technologies* (pp. 155–164). University Park, PA: ACM.

Hansen, D. L., Shneiderman, B., & Smith, M. (2010). *Analyzing social media networks with NodeXL: Insights from a connected world.* Burlington, MA: Morgan Kaufmann Publishers.

Hargadon, S. (2009). *Educational networking: The important role Web 2.0 will play in education.* (pp. 1–8). Elluminate. Retrieved from http://www.scribd.com/doc/24161189/Educational-Networking-The-Important-Role-Web-2-0-Will-Play-in-Education

Hargadon, S. (n.d.) *Classroom 2.0 Workshops: Welcome!* Retrieved March 12, 2010, from http:// workshops.classroom20.com/index.html.

Jackson, A. (2010). *Some schools advising teachers to limit texting, social networking with students.* Times-News. Twin-Falls, Idaho. Retrieved February 7, 2010 from http://www. allbusiness.com/education-training/education-administration-school-boards/13875272-1.html

Johnson, B. (2009). Wikipedia approaches its limits. *The Guardian.* London, United Kingdom. Retrieved August 12, 2009 from http://www.guardian.co.uk/technology/2009/aug/12/ wikipedia-deletionist-inclusionist

Koch, M., & Fusco, J. (2008). Designing for growth: Enabling communities of practice to develop and extend their work online. In *Communities of Practice: Creating Learning Environments for Educators* (vol. 2, pp. 1–23). Charlotte, NC: Information Age Publishing (IAP).

Kuntz, T. (2009). Idea of the day: Must reads from the NY Times Week in Review Staff. *A Writing Revolution.* New York Times Week in Review. Retrieved October 22, 2009, from http://ideas. blogs.nytimes.com/2009/10/22/a-writing-revolution/

Labi, S. (2010, March 28). Schools can sue parents. *Sunday Telegraph (Australia),* 11 Australia.

Lave, J., & Wenger, E. (1991). *Situated learning: legitimate peripheral participation.* New York: Cambridge University Press.

Li, C., & Bernoff, J. (2008). *Groundswell: Winning in a world transformed by social technologies.* Boston, MA: Harvard Business Review.

Lin, N. (2001). Building a network theory of social capital. In R. Burt, K. Cook, & N. Lin (Eds.), *Social capital: Theory and Research* (pp. 3–30). New York: Aldine de Gruyter.

O'Reilly, T. (2005). What Is Web 2.0 – design patterns and business models for the next generation of software. *Tim O'Reilly Blog.* O'Reilly Media. Retrieved September 30, 2005, from http:// oreilly.com/pub/a/web2/archive/what-is-web-20.html?page=1

Porter, J. (2008). Designing for the Social Web. Berkeley, CA: New Riders Press.

Preece, J., & Shneiderman, B. (2009). The Reader-to-Leader Framework: motivating technology-mediated social participation. *AIS Transactions on Human-Computer Interaction, 1*(1), 13–32.

Ren, Y., Kraut, R., & Kiesler, S. (2007). Applying common identity and bond theory to design of online communities. *Organization Studies, 28*(3), 377–408.

Resnick, P. (2002). Beyond bowling together: SocioTechnical capital. In J. Carroll (Ed.), *Human-computer interaction in the new millennium* (pp. 247–272). New York, NY; Boston MA: Addison-Wesley.

Tomlinson, C. A. (August, 2000). Differentiation of Instruction in the Elementary Grades. ERIC Digest. ERIC Clearinghouse on Elementary and Early Childhood Education. Retrieved August, 2000, from http://www.ericdigests.org/2001-2/elementary.html.

United States Department of Education. (2010). *National Education Technology Plan.* Office of Educational Technology, U.S. Department of Education. Retrieved from http://www.ed.gov/technology/netp-2010.

Wenger, E., White, N., & Smith, J. D. (2009). *Digital habitats: stewarding technology for communities* (1st ed.). Portland, OR: CPsquare.

Wenger, E. C., & Snyder, W. M. (2000). Communities of Practice: The Organizational Frontier. *Harvard Business Review, 78*(1), 139-145.

What Can Technology Learn from the Brain?

David H. Rose and Scott Lapinski

Much of this book, like most writing on educational technology, focuses on what we can learn from technology. This chapter takes the opposite point of view: what technology can learn from us. We have chosen this contrarian route for several reasons. First, as educators who develop technology (both of us work at CAST, on educational research and development organization), we are always looking for ways to develop better learning technologies. At least for the present, there is no better learning (or teaching) technology than the human brain, so we are continually looking at how the brain goes about the tasks of learning and teaching. What can we, as educators who design technology, learn about better design from the ways in which our own brains are designed?

We will hardly be exhaustive here; our purpose is only to illustrate several among the most obvious things about the ways that brains learn. We hope, nonetheless, to raise some issues of significance for our peers and for ourselves. We will begin with a striking syndrome that, in its anomaly, reveals several important things about the way the brain works.

A Disconnect: The Capgras Delusion

The Capgras delusion is one of the rarest and most colorful syndromes in neurology. The most striking feature of the disorder is that the patient – who is usually quite mentally lucid in other respects – comes to regard close acquaintances, typically either his parents, children, spouse, or siblings, as 'imposters,' i.e., he may claim that the person in question "looks like" or is even "identical to" his father, but really isn't. (Hirstein & Ramachandran, 1997)

Individuals with Capgras syndrome are among the most striking of patients to show up at any psychiatrist's office. Their problem sounds like a bad movie script:

D.H. Rose (✉)
CAST, Wakefield, MA, USA
e-mail: DRose@cast.org

T. Gray and H. Silver-Pacuilla (eds.), *Breakthrough Teaching and Learning:*
How Educational and Assistive Technologies are Driving Innovation,
DOI 10.1007/978-1-4419-7768-7_4, © Springer Science+Business Media, LLC 2011

they report that an alien or imposter has replaced a loved one. The imposter or alien *looks* exactly the same as their loved one, but they are sure that it is not. The "illusion" is both vivid and persistent – and quite distressing to the loved one who is, of course, really just the same (Abumrad & Krulwich, 2010).

Formerly treated as a psychiatric disorder, modern researchers now recognize that individuals with Capgras syndrome have a neurological disorder: a lesion in their brain disturbs the connection between two normally connected regions of the brain (Hirstein & Ramachandran, 1997). The resulting disorder, for our purposes, is a vivid demonstration of an important aspect of the way the brain works and learns: the brain, at least the normal brain, typically has multiple ways of "knowing." Under normal circumstances, these multiple ways of knowing are connected and integrated. What Capgras syndrome demonstrates is what happens in the odd circumstance when they are not. Let us explain.

The most obvious way that we recognize people is by their visual features. Many research studies have demonstrated that a specific region (often called the visual face form area or *fusiform gyrus*) in the temporal lobe learns to respond consistently to the distinctive features of individual faces (McCarthy, Puce, Gore, & Allison, 1997). That is, it recognizes them. But recent research has demonstrated that there are also other ways that our brains learn to respond distinctively to individual faces. One of the most interesting emerges in a different area of the brain, the limbic system, where the nervous system responds with emotion rather than vision. When a familiar face, one that evokes feelings of one type or another, is presented, this part of the brain responds with distinctive (although often subtle or unconscious) signs of emotional arousal in sweat glands, pupil dilation, heart rate, breathing, etc. Scientists are beginning to realize that we recognize individuals not only by their visual features but by the emotions they engender in us (Ellis & Lewis, 2001). We recognize someone in part by how they make us feel.

In someone with Capgras syndrome, the visual way of knowing is "disconnected" from the emotional, visceral way of knowing. As a result, they do not match up. The person looks like Tom, but does not "feel" like him.

What is most amazing is what the brain does next. Apparently when faced with two competing realities – someone who looks exactly like your wife but does not feel exactly like her – the brain seems to construct something entirely new, something that integrates the two realities into one. There are many other instances of this, the famous McGurk effect when there is a mismatch between what is seen with what is heard, visual illusions where the brain will see two different views, but only one at a time, etc. (McGurk & MacDonald, 1976).

Of what significance is this bizarre condition to educators or technology designers? Actually, there are many important things that Capgras syndrome reveals about the brain. For our purposes, we will emphasize only three. First, for constructivists like us, it is one of the more vivid demonstrations of how much the brain "constructs" the reality in which it lives, rather than simply perceiving it. Designers who think their job is merely to transfer information from the environment into a receptive, and passive, brain should take note.

Second, the Capgras syndrome illustrates how important emotion and affect is in what we know and learn. Many educational designers think of the brain as merely an information processor and their task as informational design. But that neglects the lesson of Capgras. The brain is always, constantly and pervasively, evaluating the significance or value of any information. The brain is not really an information-processing device; the Capgras delusion, and our own emotions, reveal that much of it is a values-processing device (Damasio, 1999; LeDoux, 1996).

But the larger point we want to illustrate with Capgras is that the brain has multiple ways of knowing. Usually, these ways of knowing are congruent and integrated – normally we construct, and live in, a single universe. It takes an unusual anomaly, like the Capgras delusion, to reveal the underlying diversity in the ways that we know our world.

But how many ways of knowing are there? To a neuroscientist, there are many, many ways of knowing: it has been often estimated that there are at least 30 different ways of knowing within the visual system alone (Banich, 2004). In the next section, we look at some very simple anatomy with an eye to identifying the most general ways of knowing that are distinguished in our brains.

Something Different: The Spinal Cord

One of the most obvious things about the brain is that it has many different parts.

Even the most cursory comparison of those different parts – for example, a comparison of the thalamus, the cortex, and the amygdala – under a microscope shows that they are each composed of very different and distinctively shaped neurons and those are in turn connected by very different wiring patterns. On the face of it, it seems very unlikely that each of these different parts would perform in the same way, or learn in the same way. But most of the brain is composed of three highly general components (Cytowic, 1996; Rose & Meyer, 2002). To illustrate them, we would like to take a quick look at the spinal cord, where they are easy to see.

In Fig. 1, a diagram of the circuitry of the spinal cord, you can see that there are three primary components or types of neurons: a sensory neuron, a motor neuron, and an interneuron. This is as simple as the nervous system circuitry gets. One other aspect of the circuitry is important to note: the location of each of the three types of neurons (this will be helpful later). The sensory neurons are always in the back of the nervous system – here in the back of the spinal cord. The motor neurons, in contrast, are always in the front of the nervous system (here the spinal cord). The interneurons, finally, are in the center or core of the nervous system (Stiles, 2008).

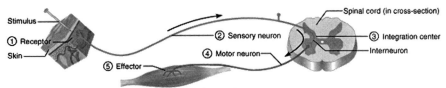

Copyright © 2001 Benjamin Cummings, an imprint of Addison Wesley Longman, Inc.

Fig. 1 Circuitry of the spinal cord

As educators, we do not usually work directly with the spinal cord or its neurons. We only introduced it here to illustrate a simple framework around which the whole brain is organized. Now we will move to a much more interesting part of the brain that educators *should* work directly with – the cerebral cortex. While the cerebral cortex is much more complicated than the spinal cord, it is basically organized in the same way.

We all recognize the cerebral cortex as the massive crinkled lobes of our brain that are mostly visible on the surface and that are the most "human" of the brain's many structures. Even within that one type of brain tissue, however, there are many distinctly specialized regions. While the specializations often seem complicated to the novice, at the most basic level they follow the same pattern that we just saw in the spinal cord. Let us elaborate on three broad types of cerebral cortex and the roles they play in learning.

Recognition Networks

First, consider the large expanse of cerebral cortex in the rear of the brain (most of what is known as parietal, occipital, and temporal lobes). That entire region of cortex is specialized for gathering, comparing, and interpreting information that comes from the senses (note the parallel to the spinal cord where sensory neurons are always found in the rear as well). For convenience, we call these regions *recognition networks* (For more information on recognition networks, see: Banich, 2004; Cabeza & Kingstone, 2001; Farah, 2000; Martin, 2007; Mountcastle, 1998).

At any given moment, we see, hear, smell, taste, and touch countless patterns – patterns of light, sound, chemicals, touch – in our environment. The posterior regions of cortex – recognition networks – are specialized for learning to perceive and understand those patterns. With time and experience, they learn to recognize the differing patterns of the smell of gasoline or coffee and make good choices about which one to have for breakfast and which one to put in the lawnmower. Learning to recognize things – to build useable knowledge about the world in which you live – is one very powerful type of learning in the brain. But there are two more.

Strategic Networks

Just as the recognition networks are specialized for gathering information from the senses, the strategic networks are specialized for action, for movement. (Again, note the parallel to spinal cord where motor neurons are in the front.) At any given moment, there are many possible courses of action an individual might take. Strategic networks are specialized for choosing what to do (setting a goal), formulating a plan or strategy for doing it, and then activating the right sequence of muscle movements to actually take action. None of those abilities come easily; the brain must learn how to set realistic goals, how to choose effective plans of action, and how to monitor progress – what are called "executive functions." And the development of those executive functions depends upon the prior mastery of many "lower level" skills and abilities which are necessary for carrying them out – learning to be fluent and automatized with millions of movements and actions (including very complicated expressive acts like speaking and writing) that can be combined and recombined again and again (For more information on strategic networks, see: Dawson & Guare, 2010; Goldberg, 2002; Jeannerod, 1997; Meltzer, 2007; Rothi & Heilman, 1997; Stuss & Knight, 2002).

Affective Networks

The third major division of the brain is not devoted to recognizing information or generating actions but to setting priorities. Since we are constantly receiving information and have many possible courses of action, we are constantly assigning values and significance to each of them, whether negative or positive. When a stranger approaches us, we immediately (and largely unconsciously) evaluate their significance: are they enticing, boring, frightening? That evaluation is critical in determining our priorities – will we ignore them (to do something else of higher priority), attend to them cautiously, approach them warmly, or run. Affective networks are critical in making that determination. To do so they combine information about the "external" environment (e.g., "Who is that approaching me?" and "What experience have I had with them or people like them in the past,") with information about our own "internal" environment (e.g., "What are my priorities right now? How hungry am I? How anxious or frightened am I from when I was mugged last year?"). Affective networks are the important part of our brain for "coloring" our experience, for giving it value and importance, for setting our priorities. We experience the work of the affective networks as motivation and emotion. Over time and experience, affective networks learn to attach motivation and emotion to the experiences of our lives (For more information on affective networks, see: Barsalou, Breazeal, & Smith, 2007; Coch, Dawson, & Fischer, 2007; Damásio, 1994; Davidson, Scherer, & Goldsmith, 2003; Easton & Emery, 2005; Lane, Nadel, & Ahern, 2000; Levesque et al., 2004; Lewis & Stieben, 2004; Rolls, 1999).

At this point, it is useful to return to the Capgras delusion as a summary of where we have been. Now, it is easy to see that Capgras results from a separation between two kinds of knowledge: what the recognition system knows and what the affective system knows. When we recognize faces, we certainly use visual cortex to do so. But we also use affective cortex to recognize how we feel about those faces, what significance they have for us. Knowing about the three basic networks, one should prompt us, however, to ask whether the third component – strategic systems – also has any role in face recognition. Good question!

Yes they do. And hopefully you will not be surprised to find that their role is focused on action and strategy rather than sensation or affect. In brief, strategic cortex knows a face by *how* it looks at it. To recognize a face requires more than a single global glance: it requires a careful, deliberate inspection of the most distinctive features (Farah, 2000). Even though this feels automatic to us, eye movement studies reveal how strategically and skillfully the eye investigates the distinctive features and relationships of the face. And, not surprisingly, strategic systems move the eyes to concentrate not only on the features that are optimal for recognizing the face (who it is), but also on the features that are optimal for recognizing the emotion in that face (what she/he means to me) (Hirstein & Ramachandran, 1997).

Why is this tripartite brain important to the work of educational technology designers? Some readers will recognize that these three brain systems underlie the three principles of universal design for learning (UDL) (Rose & Meyer, 2002). But we shall have more to say about that later. For now it is important simply to recognize one conclusion: you can never really teach (or learn) one thing in isolation. The brain is inevitably learning – all the time – in all three of the ways we have been describing. Although technology developers may think they are teaching one thing – the causes of the Civil War, say – learners are actually learning multiple things. When shown a historical paragraph, they are not only learning to *recognize* its meaning, they are learning *strategies* for how to examine future historical tracts, and they are learning how they *feel* about this content (and probably about themselves, about historical inquiry more generally, and many other things). They are learning what its personal significance is, so that they will know how to engage or disengage in the future.

This is important for many reasons, not the least of which is related to the relationship between affect and other kinds of learning. Most designers recognize the value of engagement and expend considerable effort in designing a learning environment that attracts and sustains attention. Fewer recognize, however, the pernicious effects that such designs may have long-term, when they are unconnected – or wrongly connected to actual learning goals (Lepper & Greene, 1975; Lepper, Corpus, & Iyengar, 2005). Providing external rewards and attractions to engage and sustain effort can appear to improve performance in the short run but can actually decrease the long-term motivation to learn in the relevant domain. Fabulously engaging games can boost phonics skills, but students may be learning nothing about the joy of reading and may actually read less as a result.

Educational designers typically focus too much on what recognition systems do and too little on teaching the strategies that students need for future learning. They also pay too little attention to the affective domain, that is, on designs that engage and build motivation for future learning. Game designers usually do the opposite. They focus primarily on amplifying the engagement – some would say addiction – of the environment (Gentile, 2009). They may build strategies or skills but often in domains that have little transfer to real life. The informational domain (i.e., the recognition network) is usually attended to the least. What we need are educational environments that are focused on all three: developing valuable knowledge, skills, and emotions.

It is time to take a more specific look at what the brain might teach us about the actual art or science of teaching. To do that, we want to look more closely at two important findings within the strategic networks specifically.

A Reflection of Purpose: Mirror Neurons

One of the most striking, and revolutionary, discoveries about the brain during the last decade has been the discovery of "mirror neurons." A recent scholarly review by Brass and Rüschemeyer (2010) accurately captures the importance of their discovery for many neuroscientists and cognitive psychologists. When mirror neurons were first discovered, scientists were studying how the brain controls voluntary movement. They inserted tiny electrodes deep into motor cortex (part of the strategic networks described above) to measure the activity of single motor neurons. They quickly found neurons that emitted a burst of firing whenever the monkey made a specific purposeful movement – like taking a sip from a straw. What was more dramatic, and much more surprising, was that the same neuron would also exhibit a burst of firing when the monkey merely *observed* another monkey making the same action. In that sense, these neurons seemed to "mirror" the behavior performed by another.

Many studies have been conducted since, which speculate on the meaning of this neural "mirroring." Recent research has shown, for example, that mirror neurons do not just reflect simple actions; they reflect their *purpose*. That is, a mirror neuron that emits a burst of activity when the monkey observes another monkey reaching out to grab a raisin, does not emit that same burst when the same monkey reaches out (in the same way) to turn a knob (Rizzolatte & Sinigaglia, 2007). Mirror neurons thus seem to reflect not only the physical actions of others, but also their goals and intentions.

With these kinds of properties, scientists have indulged in considerable speculation about the role of mirror neurons. Many have speculated, for example, that this mirroring capacity is essential for *understanding* the actions of others (Rizzolatte & Sinigaglia, 2007). Individuals understand the actions of others because they are able to "simulate" or mirror those actions in their own heads. That is how the *meaning* of actions is recognized, assimilated, and understood.

Not surprisingly, many scientists have concluded that this mirroring functionality is also the basis for *imitation*. With the ability to mirror actions produced by others, it is possible not only to understand them but also to imitate or copy them. This is not a trivial matter for any brain. While monkeys, and humans, are skilled at learning by imitation, most animals do not in fact have that capacity. As many neuroscientists see it, the functionality of mirror neurons is one of the essential substrates for learning by imitation (Iacoboni & Dapretto, 2006).

For "altricial" species – like humans and primates – that depend for their survival on learning rather than inherited fixed action patterns, there is a premium on "social" learning, the ability to learn from the experience of others. The protracted dependency of these species on their caregivers – in contrast to "precocial" species that are independent almost from birth – provides both the opportunity and necessity for the advantages of imitation. For many scientists, mirror neurons are one of the brain's best mechanisms for taking advantage of what others have already learned.

There is one more dramatic development in the last few years of research on mirror neurons that is important for this discussion. While mirror neurons were discovered in motor cortex, recent research has found this same mirroring capacity in many other areas of the human brain – including all three of the major networks we have discussed earlier. Recently, the scientists who originally discovered mirror neurons in motor cortex have published a book with a remarkably more expansive title that reflects the wider findings: *Mirrors in the Brain: How Our Minds Share Actions, Emotions, and Experience* (Rizzolatte & Sinigaglia, 2007). Note the close resemblance, with slight name changes, to the three networks as outlined in this chapter.

In this new, expanded view of mirror neurons, scientists believe that the mirroring functionality is not only the key for understanding motor action and imitation, but also for understanding the highest forms of human cognition and social behavior. Through these capacities – resident in affective and recognition cortex rather than just in motor cortex – humans gain the power for understanding emotions, for "theory of mind," for empathy, and for compassion (Rizzolatte & Sinigaglia, 2007). All of these depend on the ability to mirror or simulate not only what another person is doing, but also what they are feeling, what they are thinking, and what they know about or care about.

In summary, many now believe that mirroring capacity underlies much of what makes us human. Indeed, our very culture (and certainly our entertainment) depends upon the ability to effectively mirror and understand the social and emotional behavior of other humans.

It is not hard to see the relevance of mirroring for educational designers. At the very least, it encourages all of us to take advantage of what mirror neurons can do. That is to say, to maximize the opportunities for students to learn not by trial and error, nor even by independent exploration and discovery (although some of that is very good), but by taking advantage of the capacity for imitation.

Clearly, imitation has been a critical aspect of most forms of mentoring and apprenticeships over the span of human history. The arrival of "book learning" altered the landscape profoundly, and privileged a different method of learning – one based on the transfer of information. While there is value in that kind of learning, the drastic reduction in active apprenticeships – with lots of opportunities for modeling and imitation – fails to take advantage of the mirroring that our brains can do.

New technologies provide a much better platform for taking advantage of modeling and imitating than textbooks (Dalton & Proctor, 2007; Rose & Dalton, 2009). Although real, live skillful teachers would be better under most circumstances than anything computers can do, however, real, live skillful teachers are only intermittently available to their students. The problems of time sharing with 20–30 students simultaneously are obvious.

The popularity of "How to" videos on YouTube is testimony to how much more effective this medium can be for mentoring and modeling than the printed word. More importantly, many research studies have investigated the advantages of providing "just in time" modeling by human mentors on video or by avatars created on computers. Game designers have essentially abandoned instruction manuals or written descriptions of rules of play because the ability of new media to model intended behavior is so much more powerful and direct (Gee, 2007). Instructional designers who are using modern technologies should take full advantage of both the technology's capability for modeling and the brains capability for mirroring. They should also take care to consider modeling that addresses all three of the networks – modeling of affective skills and effective strategies for managing frustration, for instance, is as important as modeling skills for finding the lowest common denominator.

A Key to Learning: Pervasive and Reciprocal Feedback

Most descriptions or drawings of the motor systems in the brain emphasize the giant motor neurons in motor cortex that travel all the way down the spinal cord to where they synapse on "lower" motor neurons (Stiles, 2008). From those lower motor neurons, a long axon snakes far out of the spinal cord to connect to actual muscles in the arms and legs. The emphasis on motor neurons makes sense because they are the active link between our brain and our ability to move and act upon the world. But anatomists, those who study the brain's biological structure, typically note something else about the motor system: the overwhelming pervasiveness of mechanisms for "feedback."

The nervous system is not composed primarily of simple one-way connections from brain to muscles. Instead, the connections between brain and muscle are highly reciprocal. Indeed, the majority of the connections in the motor system are reciprocal: they are not merely conveying impulses from the brain to the muscles but are carrying information from muscles (and other neurons and parts of the body) back to the brain (Banich, 2004; Jeannerod, 1997). From the architecture, it is clear that the brain does not merely issue orders to move muscles, making actions possible: it collects information about the status of those muscles and the effects of its own manipulation of them. The brain is constantly monitoring the effects of its own activity (Dawson & Guare, 2010; Goldberg, 2002; Rothi & Heilman, 1997; Stuss & Knight, 2002). While the brain's motor neurons are often the most highlighted aspects of the motor system, the anatomy suggests how important feedback is to its success.

Observation of the anatomy and physiology reveals something else about feedback. In the discussion so far, we have highlighted only the *motor* feedback, the feedback that is localized within the motor systems themselves. But the wiring of the nervous system reveals other feedback channels as well, feedback from very different parts of the nervous system. Indeed, both of the large network systems described earlier – recognition networks and affective networks – provide extensive and continuous feedback to the strategic motor systems. A few words about the nature of their feedback is warranted.

Recognition networks are wired to provide feedback from the senses, not from muscles. That feedback – from effects on the environment that can be seen, heard, touched, tasted – is critical in determining not just whether an action was success-fully launched, but whether it achieved its intended results (Banich, 2004; Cabeza & Kingstone, 2001; Farah, 2000; Martin, 2007; Mountcastle, 1998). The infor-mation from the senses does not tell us about whether muscles properly con-tracted or flexed but rather whether the pounding of the hammer actually hit the nail, whether the cup actually reach the lips, whether the pitched ball was a strike, and whether the beating of the drum was forceful enough to be heard above the orchestra.

The feedback from affective networks serves a very different function. The feed-back is not about whether movements achieved the *physical* results intended but whether they achieved the *emotional or affective* results desired (Barsalou et al., 2007; Coch et al., 2007; Damásio, 1994). Did the hammering of the nail bring *pain* (perhaps because you were hammering your thumb) rather than satisfaction, did the cup of coffee taste *good*, did the sound of the drum bring *pleasure*? This affective kind of feedback is essential, especially to learning, because it motivates and priori-tizes future actions. Where other feedback compares results to what was intended, this kind of feedback compares results to what is *valued*, to the goals and priorities the individual holds. Such feedback helps to determine whether actions are valued – either positively or negatively – enough to be repeated, avoided, prioritized, practiced, or even obsessed about. Much cognitive neuroscience research about memory, attention, and persistence has emphasized the critical role of emotion and affective feedback in facilitating (or inhibiting) learning (Kensinger, 2004; Levine & Pizarro, 2004).

What significance does all of this – the enormous and diversified investment of neural architecture to feedback – have for the work of educational designers? What it suggests to us is how important feedback is to successful learning. The brain, essentially wired for learning, is demonstrably wired for feedback. In comparison, most educational environments seem grossly impoverished in the quality, density, immediacy, and variety of feedback they provide. The core procedures and activi-ties of most classrooms provide little feedback (to either teacher or student) or provide feedback that is too infrequent, too late, or too uninformative (Blackwell, Trzesniewski, & Dweck, 2007; Cimpian, Arce, Markman, & Dweck, 2007). For example, textbooks are completely disabled in this regard. They are presentational (feed-forward) only. As a result, tests or exercises are added to supplement the read-ing, but those are usually summative rather than formative, neither timely nor informative enough to guide instruction or learning. They simply do not provide the feedback that the brain seems eager and prepared to receive.

The new technologies of learning provide a better, or at least more promising, platform. Unlike textbooks, modern technology has the capacity to be dynamic, interactive, and responsive. As such, with proper design, new learning technolo-gies can provide feedback that is plentiful, varied, and timely. But too often new technologies are designed more like textbooks, with only limited options for feedback, options that are far narrower than the nervous system is prepared for.

As a guide to what kinds of feedback should be considered, it is useful to consider each of the three networks. First, consider the strategic networks and especially their motor capabilities. We are all aware of the advances in the design of information technologies so that they provide basic sensory–motor feedback. Computer keyboards, automated teller machines, cell phones all tend to give immediate feedback – a tactile click, a physical depression, a beep, a visual cue – to let us know that our action was registered. Designers have long ago learned how frustrated and lost customers feel when they do not get that feedback.

But of course that kind of feedback is hardly enough. Knowing that a key or button was successfully pushed is necessary but not sufficient. We also need feedback on whether our motor acts achieved the results on the environment we intended – did we actually type the password with letters in the right order, did we choose the multiple choice answer that was correct, did we generate a good synthesis of the data from our experiment, did our essay or e-mail convey a proper tone of sarcasm. All of this kind of feedback requires recognition cortex – the ability to perceive the results of our actions and make sense of them, as well as the ability to compare our actual effects on the environment (including whatever we create) to what we intended.

Most new learning technologies do not provide enough of this kind of feedback. But there are excellent models available. Many "smart" games, of course, provide this kind of feedback consistently and continuously. In fact, many cognitive psychologists have surmised that one of the most important reasons that games are so addictive and motivating is that they are rich and immediate with their feedback (Gee, 2007; Shaffer, 2006). Some well-designed educational programs take similar advantage of the power of technology to provide pervasive feedback, but their purposes and techniques are much more instructional. That is, they track what students actually do, provide helpful feedback – to both students and designers – based on the kinds of errors that student's exhibit, and modify instruction on the basis of that feedback. For examples, see the chapter on adaptive assessments by Russell (this volume).

Finally, let us consider feedback in terms of the affective networks. The work of Carol Dweck, Deci, and many others have demonstrated how powerful the right kind of emotional feedback can be for motivating learning, and how motivationally unproductive the wrong kind can be (Blackwell et al., 2007; Cimpian et al., 2007; Deci & Moller, 2005; Dweck, 2000). Much of what passes for educational technology rewards students in the ways that researchers have demonstrated to be unproductive, an easy thing to fix. More challenging is to design educational technologies so that they can not only monitor actions and their results, but also their affective consequences as well.

Good teachers are constantly monitoring their student's affect and motivation in order to make optimal instructional decisions and to provide the right kind of feedback. They continually monitor a student's level of interest, frustration, boredom, anticipation, anxiety, to decide when to push harder, when to modify the difficulty, when to congratulate, when to take a break. So far, modern learning technologies are drastically less capable of this kind of affective monitoring than are experienced teachers, but interesting work is being done that demands attention (Picard, 2010; Woolf et al., 2009).

This last point bears emphasis. Most cognitive psychologists and noneducators think of teaching as "informational work" – the work inherent in dispensing information or teaching specific skills. But experienced educators – and neuroscientists, if they think about it – know that teaching is as much or more "emotional work." Effective teaching requires the ability to understand exactly where students are in their learning – not only what information and skills they have but also the frustration, boredom, anticipation, wonder, and passion they are feeling. Effectively optimizing the emotional conditions for learning is the most important challenge of teaching. Educational technologies have a lot to learn in this area.

Anxiety and Individual Differences

One of the most obvious things about human brains is how much they all look alike. The overall shape and fissured lobes of the cerebral cortex looks pretty much the same from one to another. But modern techniques for imaging the brain have made it possible to vividly illuminate the microscopic anatomy of the living brain and even to watch the microphysiology and chemistry of its dynamic activity. What is equally obvious is that each brain is strikingly unique and individual (Hariri, 2009; Leonard, Eckert, Given, Virginia, & Eden, 2006). No two are alike.

How are they different? In almost every way one can measure: in gross anatomy (i.e., the relative size and shape of various regions), in fine structural anatomy (the detailed pattern of connections between cells), in physiology, and in chemistry.

These individual differences in the brain's anatomy, physiology, and chemistry are as distinctive as the differences in individual fingerprints. But the effects of those differences are much greater. Researchers repeatedly discover dramatic relationships between the anatomical and physiological differences in the brain and many aspects of behavior, from the simplest to the most complex (Hariri, 2009).

Consider just one example: individual differences in anxiety. Whether measured behaviorally (e.g., by observation or self-report) or physiologically (e.g., blood pressure, heart rate, skin conductance, etc.), individuals vary significantly in both their chronic level of anxiety and in their reactivity to potentially stressful situations. Some people are consistently much more anxious than others. What is interesting is that those behavioral differences can be predicted on the basis of measurable differences in the brain's anatomy and physiology (van Reekum et al., 2007). For example, researchers have found that the *volume* of brain tissue in the amygdala (but not most other areas of the brain) is correlated with the level of trait anxiety reported by the individual – the smaller the volume of the amygdala on the left side of the brain, the more anxious the individual (Spampinato, Wood, De Simone, & Grafman, 2009).

It is clear that this one difference would have profound effects on learning: some children will be too anxious for the social and cognitive demands of learning in almost any classroom situation, some will not be nearly anxious enough. Others will be profoundly affected (either positively or negatively) by unexpected stressors at home or school.

Anxiety is but one dimension of individual differences that have been linked to brain differences – there are hundreds of others. By the time kids go to school, they have brains that are really different from one another – differences that are founded in biology and continually reshaped by the environment. These differences are not subtle or ephemeral – they reflect substantial differences in who the learner is.

What is the lesson from all this and what are the implications for educational designers? First, it is important to recognize that most publishers and educational technology developers do not design as if their users differ significantly one from the other. For the most part, educational designs are almost completely uniform, with minor modifications (occasionally) for individuals with disabilities. Given the brain's great interindividual differences, it seems that technology developers might take more advantage of the flexibility of technology to differentiate along the lines of individual differences. But what kinds of differences are worth designing for?

The UDL Guidelines

The field of UDL has grown up around a common framework for recognizing the full extent of individual differences and for addressing them in the design of curricula. The UDL guidelines demonstrate what might be done to improve the one-size-fits-all curriculum that has been traditionally used in schools (Rose & Gravel, 2009). These guidelines are organized into three principles that directly correlate to the three brain networks described in this chapter. The principles help to articulate the kinds of options that are important to consider in designing a curriculum that is effective when students, as they always are, are diverse. (For a detailed description of the guidelines, please visit http://www.udlcenter.org/.) Here are the three principles with a brief orientation to them.

Principle I: Provide Multiple Means of Representation

This principle addresses the diversity that would be typically associated with recognition networks of the brain. It is important to provide options for students for perception, language and symbols, and comprehension. Perception is the most basic level of this principle. Students need to have physical access to the information. This could mean customizing the display by increasing text size or providing students with a text to speech option. Simply providing an unsupported text or an audio recording is not enough for most students to really comprehend the information presented. Consideration must be given to the diversity of preferences and limitations between learners.

The next step in providing multiple means of representation is to ensure that all students can access the language and symbols that are being used. This step recognizes that not all students have the same linguistic backgrounds. Beyond just language, students differ in their understanding of vocabulary, fluency, language structure, and mathematical symbols. Some suggestions in this area include: preteaching vocabulary, making relationships between symbols explicit, and providing glossaries with pronunciation guides.

Finally, to truly include all students, options must be given for comprehension. Students do not all understand in the same way. This is because each individual brings a unique set of knowledge and experience; so do not learn in the same ways. This option includes: activating background knowledge, highlighting relationships, guiding information processing, and supporting memory and transfer. Some ways to do these things are activating background knowledge, using graphic organizers, scaffolding instruction, and giving sufficient time for thinking.

Principle II: Provide Multiple Means of Action and Expression

This is the "how" of learning, and falls into the strategic networks. It involves providing options for physical action, expressive skills and fluency, and executive functions. The simplest level to provide options for is physical action. It goes without saying that students need physical access to the curriculum. This could include things like ensuring there are multiple ways to respond (not just typing or handwriting) or allowing students to use navigations tools or assistive technologies.

The next level is providing options for expressive skills and fluency. All students differ in their proficiency in particular media. Some might be very familiar with using a computer, while some have very limited experiences. Options should be provided for learners in regards to what type of media they use, the tools they can use to help themselves, and how to scaffold their practice. This could include allowing students to use spell check or giving appropriate feedback to students.

The most important level in this principle is providing options for executive functions. As previously noted in the section on strategic networks, executive functions are vital to learning. Learners need to set a goal, make a plan, execute the plan, and evaluate whether they were successful or not. This involves a great deal of organization and planning, something not everyone can do easily. It is therefore important to support each of the aforementioned aspects of executive functioning. To do this one might use models, scaffolding, checklists, embedded prompts, mentors, and a variety of other strategies.

Principle III: Provide Multiple Means of Engagement

In this principle, the "why" of learning is addressed through the affective networks. One must provide options for recruiting interest, sustaining effort and persistence, and self-regulation. All of these options are more difficult to implement because they involve accounting for students emotions. The physical environment can be changed easily, but this is more difficult to accomplish. However, it is affect that regulates all learning.

Options should be provided for recruiting interest. This might include something as simple as giving students choice and removing potential distractions to allowing students to develop their own goals. It is also important that goals and purposes are genuine. Most likely students will not be overly excited about doing busy work. They want meaning and purpose to be varied. Worksheets become trite and ordinary when only worksheets are used.

It is equally important to ensure that all students are persistent and effortful in their work. This means that goals must be made clear, demands and resources should be varied to optimize challenge, collaboration and community should be fostered, and feedback should be provided. Students need to understand what they are doing, and if what they are doing is accurate or not. Again, they need meaning and purpose.

Finally, options need to be provided for self-regulation. In many ways, this is the ultimate goal of all education. Learners will leave teachers and gain independence. Teachers cannot always be there to give support and make accommodations. Options need to be given to allow students to develop their own goals and expectations, coping skills and strategies, and reflection and assessment skills. Many of these goals revolve around helping students, through scaffolding and modeling, understand their strengths and weaknesses as learners. With this knowledge, they can better know how to support themselves without the help of a teacher.

Conclusion

The human brain's capacity – and its design – for learning are unique, easily distinguishable from any other learning device in the animal kingdom or the world of new technology. In this paper, we have highlighted a few notable aspects of the way the human brain learns, aspects that we think merit consideration by all those who develop learning technologies. Our list is hardly exhaustive, and there is much to learn.

We wish to end, however, with a different observation. While we can train animals and computers to do astonishingly complex tasks, to play chess, for example, we have not been able to successfully train either animals or computers to be competent teachers (we can program them to do teacherly things, but the underlying pedagogy and technology has inevitably been designed by a human who is actually doing the teaching by proxy). It may well be that human brains differ more profoundly from other brains in their power to teach than in their power to learn. It is this unmistakably human capacity – teaching – that needs more attention in both neuroscience and education. That attention will have much to teach us about making better teaching technologies.

References

Abumrad, J., & Krulwich, R. (2010). Seeing impostors: When loved ones suddenly aren't. *NPR Series: Radiolab*. Retrieved from http://www.npr.org/templates/story/story.php?storyId=1215 66675&ft=1&f=121566675

Banich, M. T. (2004). *Cognitive neuroscience and neuropsychology*. New York, NY: Houghton Mifflin.

Barsalou, L. W., Breazeal, C., & Smith, L. B. (2007). Cognition as coordinated non-cognition. *Cognitive Processing, 8*(2), 79–91. doi:10.1007/s10339-007-0163-1.

Blackwell, L. S., Trzesniewski, K. H., & Dweck, C. S. (2007). Implicit theories of intelligence predict achievement across an adolescent transition: A longitudinal study and an intervention. *Child Development, 78*(1), 246–263. doi:10.1111/j.1467-8624.2007.00995.x.

Brass, M., & Rüschemeyer, S. (2010). Mirrors in science: How mirror neurons changed cognitive neuroscience. *Cortex, 46*(1), 139–143. doi:10.1016/j.cortex.2009.04.005.

Cabeza, R., & Kingstone, A. (2001). *Handbook of functional neuroimaging of cognition*. Cambridge, MA: MIT Press.

Cimpian, A., Arce, H. M. C., Markman, E. M., & Dweck, C. S. (2007). Subtle linguistic cues affect children's motivation. *Psychological Science, 18*(4), 314–316. doi:10.1111/j.1467-9280. 2007.01896.x.

Coch, D., Dawson, G., & Fischer, K. W. (Eds.). (2007). *Human behavior, learning, and the developing brain: Atypical development*. New York, NY: The Guilford Press.

Cytowic, R. E. (1996). *The neurological side of neuropsychology*. Cambridge, MA: The MIT Press.

Dalton, B., & Proctor, C. P. (2007). Reading as thinking: Integrating strategy instruction in a universally designed digital literacy environment. In D. S. McNamara (Ed.), *Reading comprehension strategies: Theories, interventions, and technologies* (pp. 421–439). Mahwah, NJ: Lawrence Erlbaum Assoc Inc.

Damasio, A. R. (1999). *The feeling of what happens: Body and emotion in the making of consciousness*. New York, NY: Harcourt Inc.

Damásio, A. R. (1994). *Descartes' error: Emotion, reason, and the human brain*. New York, NY: Avon Books.

Davidson, R. J., Scherer, K. R., & Goldsmith, H. H. (Eds.). (2003). *Handbook of affective sciences*. New York, NY: Oxford University Press.

Dawson, P., & Guare, R. (2010). *Executive skills in children and adolescents: A practical guide to assessment and intervention*. New York, NY: The Guilford Press.

Deci, E. L., & Moller, A. C. (2005). The concept of competence: A starting place for understanding intrinsic motivation and self-determined extrinsic motivation. In A. J. Elliot & C. S. Dweck (Eds.), *Handbook of competence and motivation* (pp. 579–597). New York, NY: The Guilford Press.

Dweck, C. S. (2000). *Self-theories: Their role in motivation, personality, and development*. Philadelphia, PA: Psychology Press.

Easton, A., & Emery, N. (Eds.). (2005). *The cognitive neuroscience of social behaviour*. Hove, UK: Psychology Press.

Ellis, H. D., & Lewis, M. B. (2001). Capgras delusion: A window on face recognition. *Trends in Cognitive Sciences, 5*(4), 149–156. doi:10.1016/S1364-6613(00)01620-X.

Farah, M. J. (2000). *The cognitive neuroscience of vision*. Malden, MA: Blackwell Publishers.

Gee, J. P. (2007). *What video games have to teach us about learning and literacy*. New York, NY: Palgrave MacMillan.

Gentile, D. (2009). Pathological video-game use among youth ages 8 to 18. *Psychological Science, 20*(5), 594–602. doi:10.1111/j.1467-9280.2009.02340.x.

Goldberg, E. (2002). *The executive brain: Frontal lobes and the civilized mind*. New York, NY: Oxford University Press.

Hariri, A. R. (2009). The neurobiology of individual differences in complex behavioral traits. *Annual Review of Neuroscience, 32*, 225–247. doi:10.1146/annurev.neuro.051508.135335.

Hirstein, W., & Ramachandran, V. S. (1997). Capgras syndrome: A novel probe for understanding the neural representation of the identity and familiarity of persons. *Proceedings of the Royal Society B: Biological Sciences, 264*(1380), 437.

Iacoboni, M., & Dapretto, M. (2006). The mirror neuron system and the consequences of its dysfunction. *Nature Reviews Neuroscience, 7*(12), 942–951. doi:10.1038/nrn2024.

Jeannerod, M. (1997). *The cognitive neuroscience of action.* Cambridge, MA: Blackwell.

Kensinger, E. A. (2004). Remembering emotional experiences: The contribution of valence and arousal. *Reviews in the Neurosciences, 15*, 241–252.

Lane, R. D., Nadel, L., & Ahern, G. L. (Eds.). (2000). *Cognitive neuroscience of emotion.* New York, NY: Oxford University Press.

LeDoux, J. E. (1996). *The emotional brain: The mysterious underpinnings of emotional life.* New York, NY: Simon & Schuster.

Leonard, C., Eckert, M., Given, B., Virginia, B., & Eden, G. (2006). Individual differences in anatomy predict reading and oral language impairments in children. *Brain, 129*(12), 3329–3342. doi:10.1093/brain/awl262.

Lepper, M. R., Corpus, J. H., & Iyengar, S. S. (2005). Intrinsic and extrinsic motivational orientations in the classroom: Age differences and academic correlates. *Journal of Educational Psychology, 97*(2), 184–196. doi:10.1037/0022-0663.97.2.184.

Lepper, M. R., & Greene, D. (1975). Turning play into work: Effects of adult surveillance and extrinsic rewards on children's intrinsic motivation. *Journal of Personality and Social Psychology, 31*(3), 479–486. doi:10.1037/h0076484.

Levesque, J., Joanette, Y., Mensour, B., Beaudoin, G., Leroux, J. M., Bourgouin, P., et al. (2004). Neural basis of emotional self-regulation in childhood. *Neuroscience, 129*(2), 361–369. doi:10.1016/j.neuroscience.2004.07.032.

Levine, L. J., & Pizarro, D. A. (2004). Emotion and memory research: A grumpy overview. *Social Cognition, 22*(5), 530–554. doi:10.1521/soco.22.5.530.50767.

Lewis, M. D., & Stieben, J. (2004). Emotion regulation in the brain: Conceptual issues and directions for developmental research. *Child Development, 75*(2), 371–376. doi:10.1111/j.1467-8624. 2004.00680.x.

Martin, A. (2007). The representation of object concepts in the brain. *Annual Review of Psychology, 58*(1), 25–45. doi:10.1146/annurev.psych.57.102904.190143.

McCarthy, G., Puce, A., Gore, J. C., & Allison, T. (1997). Face-specific processing in the human fusiform gyrus. *Journal of Cognitive Neuroscience, 9*(5), 605–610. doi:10.1162/jocn.1997.9.5.605.

McGurk, H., & MacDonald, J. (1976). Hearing lips and seeing voices. *Nature, 264*, 746–748. doi:10.1038/264746a0.

Meltzer, L. (2007). *Executive function in education: From theory to practice.* New York, NY: The Guilford Press.

Mountcastle, V. B. (1998). *Perceptual neuroscience: The cerebral cortex.* Cambridge, MA: Harvard University Press.

Picard, R. W. (2010). Emotion research by the people, for the people. *Emotion Review, 2*(3), 250–254. doi:10.1177/1754073910364256.

Rizzolatte, G., & Sinigaglia, C. (2007). Mirror neurons and motor intentionality. *Functional Neurology, 22*(4), 205–210.

Rizzolatti, G., & Sinigaglia, C. (2008). *Mirrors in the brain: How our minds share actions and emotions* (F. Anderson Trans.). New York: Oxford University Press.

Rolls, E. T. (1999). *The brain and emotion.* New York, NY: Oxford University Press.

Rose, D., & Dalton, B. (2009). Learning to read in the digital age. *Mind, Brain, and Education, 3*(2), 74–83. doi:10.1111/j.1751-228X.2009.01057.x.

Rose, D. H., & Gravel, J. W. (2009). Getting from here to there: UDL, global positioning systems, and lessons for improving education. In D. T. Gordon, J. W. Gravel, & L. A. Schifter (Eds.), *A policy reader in universal design for learning.* Cambridge, MA: Harvard Education Press.

Rose, D. H., & Meyer, A. (2002). *Teaching every student in the digital age: Universal design for learning.* Alexandria, VA: Association for Supervision and Curriculum Development.

Rothi, L. J. G., & Heilman, K. M. (1997). *Apraxia: The neuropsychology of action*. Hove, UK: Psychology Press.

Shaffer, D. W. (2006). *How computer games help children learn*. New York, NY: Palgrave Macmillan.

Spampinato, M. V., Wood, J. N., De Simone, V., & Grafman, J. (2009). Neural correlates of anxiety in healthy volunteers: A voxel-based morphometry study. *Journal of Neuropsychiatry and Clinical Neurosciences, 21*(2), 199–205. doi:10.1176/appi.neuropsych.21.2.199.

Stiles, J. (2008). *The fundamentals of brain development: Integrating nature and nurture*. Cambridge, MA: Harvard University Press.

Stuss, D. T., & Knight, R. T. (2002). *Principles of frontal lobe function*. New York, NY: Oxford University Press.

van Reekum, C. M., Urry, H. L., Johnstone, T., Thurow, M. E., Frye, C. J., Jackson, C. A., et al. (2007). Individual differences in amygdala and ventromedial prefrontal cortex activity are associated with evaluation speed and psychological well-being. *Journal of Cognitive Neuroscience, 19*(2), 237–248. doi:10.1162/jocn.2007.19.2.237.

Woolf, B., Burleson, W., Arroyo, I., Dragon, T., Cooper, D., & Picard, R. (2009). Affect-aware tutors: Recognising and responding to student affect. *International Journal of Learning Technology, 4*(3), 129–164. doi:10.1504/IJLT.2009.028804.

The Potential of Social Media for Students with Disabilities

Yong Zhao and Wei Qiu

Social media tools are vital to the lives of teenagers today. According to the 2010 study by Kaiser Family Foundation, American teenagers, aged 8–18, spend an average of 7.5 hours a day, 7 days a week using these tools (Rideout, Foehr, & Roberts, 2010). It is against this backdrop of our teenagers' avid media fascination that parents, educators, and the general public have been trying to understand and determine the best way to utilize these tools to engage students in education.

In this chapter, we present an overview of how and why social media are used around the world. This discussion is followed by an examination of the potential of social media for students with disabilities. Specifically, we explore ways that social media tools can enhance the learning and daily life experience of students with special needs and their caregivers, and how social media may be redefining talent and abilities for these students.

What Is Social Media?

As in the case of all new and emerging technologies, it is difficult to find one definition that is accepted by the majority of users. Scholars, the social media industry, and social media enthusiasts provide various definitions for social media tools. A scholarly interpretation of social media comes from a study that defines social media as "a group of Internet-based applications that allow the creation and exchange of user-generated content" (Kaplan & Haenlein, 2010). Based on this definition, typical social media tools include blogs, social network sites (SNS), virtual worlds, games, Wikipedia, YouTube, etc.

In an example of the industry's effort to capture the essence of social media, Mayfield (2008) interprets social media as "a group of emerging online media with a number of characteristics: participation, openness, conversation, community, and

Y. Zhao (✉)
University of Oregon, Portland, OR, USA
e-mail: yongzhao@uoregon.edu

T. Gray and H. Silver-Pacuilla (eds.), *Breakthrough Teaching and Learning:*
How Educational and Assistive Technologies are Driving Innovation,
DOI 10.1007/978-1-4419-7768-7_5, © Springer Science+Business Media, LLC 2011

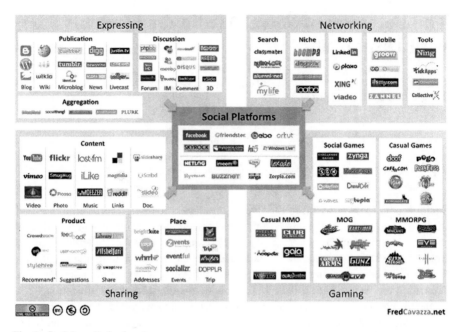

Fig. 1 Social media landscape

connectedness." This definition includes six types of tools including blogs, wikis, podcasts, forums, content communities, and microblogging (e.g., Twitter).

Fred Cavazza (2009), an independent consultant and power blogger, defines social media as a "landscape" that encompasses an extensive set of social media services and tools. He views the landscape as one that includes tweeting, tagging, and sharing by the millions who use these social media tools. According to Cavazza, the social media landscape consists of four main activities – expressing, sharing, networking, and gaming – that are structured around social platforms (Fig. 1).

The variation in definitions reveals an interesting perspective on new media tools. These tools are depicted as channels that encourage the engagement of individuals and grassroots voices rather than an authoritative voice. In addition, these definitions spotlight the use of social media tools to influence others. Teenagers interact with and influence their friends in many different ways, including through expressing opinions; sharing photos, videos, music, and other digital media; networking; and gaming. A third common theme is that social media are an extension of our physical existence (McLuhan & Gordon, 2003). If McLuhan's 1967 argument is still relevant, that "the medium is the message," then one could argue that social media send a clear and strong message that it is worthwhile to stay connected anytime, anywhere. As summarized in Table 1, Cavazza illustrates the various uses for social networking that are popular among youth today (2009).

Social media are not necessarily confined to the Internet. Mobile phones, for example, have become globally popular social media platforms that provide various

Table 1 Social media, tools, and examples

Function	Tools	Examples
Expressing	Publication tools	Blogs (blogger), wikis (wikipedia), microblogs (twitter), citizen news (digg), livecast (blogtv), texting
	Discussion tools	Forums (tianya), IM (MSN), 3D chats (IMVU), texting
	Aggregation tools	FriendFeed, etc.
Sharing	Content sharing	Video (YouTube), pictures (Flickr), music (Last.fm), links (Delicious), documents (Slideshare)
	Product sharing	Recommendation platforms (Crowdstorm, douban), collaborative feedback (FeedBack2.0), swapping platforms (LibraryThing)
	Place sharing	Local address (Whrrl), events (Upcoming), trips (TripWolf)
Networking	Ex-classmates	Classmates
	Niche networks	Boompa
	BtoB networks	LinkedIn
	Mobile networks	Groovr
	Network building	Ning
Gaming	Casual games	Pogo, BigFish
	Social games	Zynga, PlayFish, MMORPG (World of Warcraft), MMO (Drift City), Casual MMO (Club Penguin)
Platforms		Facebook, MySpace, Bebo, Orkut, Mixi, Cyworld, Xiaonei

services for communicating, the least of which is a telephone. In fact, according to a study conducted by the Pew Research Center, texting surpasses all other media activities among teenagers (Lenhart, Madden, Macgill, & Smith, 2007). As Gray et al. (this volume) make clear, "the youth of today are wired and tech-savvy;" their world is inseparable from the digital landscape.

How Social Media are Used Globally

During the emergent days of social media, researchers have noticed that teenagers' social media use varies from region to region. For example, American teenagers seemed more active on computer-based social applications, such as e-mail, chat rooms, and videogames, whereas teenagers in Japan and the Scandinavian nations were more avid adopters of mobile phone and other mobile services (Lyman, Billings, Ellinger, Finn, & Perkel, 2005).

This section summarizes the literature that compares teenagers' social media activities in the West, such as the USA and the UK, with that from the East, such as China, Japan, and South Korea. These countries are selected because individually, they are very different from each other in terms of the spread and participation with social media, and collectively, these countries more or less reflect the current "pulse" and future trends of social media around the globe.

Texting

Texting, short for text messaging, is the exchange of information between people through mobile devices or the Internet. Since its inception, texting has been rapidly adopted by teenagers worldwide and has become increasingly popular as mobile phone ownership among the young generation increases dramatically and the cost of texting becomes more affordable. In the USA, almost two out of three young people (66%) owned a cell phone in 2010, up from 39% in 2005 (Rideout et al.,). According to a 2009 Nielsen study, American teenagers on average sent 3,146 text messages a month in the fall of 2009 or 10 messages every waking hour in their after-school life (Entner, 2010). Girls tend to spend more time texting than boys, and African American and Hispanic children tend to use text messages more than their white peers.

In the UK, half of 5- to 9-year-old children own a cell phone (Naish, 2009). While there is no specific data available on how many text messages British children send on a daily basis, it is not difficult to imagine the magnitude of their activity, based on the fact that the British sent 11 million text messages an hour in 2009 (MDA, 2010).

In Asia, the cell phone penetration rate reached a record high in 2009: 48.9% in China; 77.3% in Japan; and 80.6% in South Korea, according to a study co-sponsored by GSM Association and NTT Docomo (GSMA & NTT Docomo, 2009). Available data show that 20% of Japanese high-school girls own two phones, and some own even more (Mundy, 2010). Teenagers use mobile phones mainly for texting and e-mail rather than voice calling (GSMA & NTT Docomo, 2009). Low cost might be the main reason for the popularity of texting among Asian teenagers. According to the MIIT (Ministry of Industry and Information Technology, 2006), the price for sending a message in China is 0.1 RMB (Renminbi, equivalent to U.S.$0.012), which is much cheaper than a local call (0.3 RMB/min, equivalent to U.S.$0.03) or a long-distance call (0.7 RMB/min, equivalent to U.S.$0.10).

Across the globe, teenagers use texting for a variety of purposes. In a study that explored the theme of text messaging among young people, researchers found that a majority (61%) of messages were related to relationship maintenance, such as making social arrangements; offering salutations; and maintaining friendly, romantic, and sexual relationships, while another large percentage (31%) involved exchanging information and making practical arrangements (Thurlow & Brown, 2002). However, among parents and educators, the texting mania causes serious concerns, such as text addiction, text bullying, "sexting" (sending text messages with sexual content), and inhibited literacy development (Ambrogi, 2009). And while absolute numbers of these infractions remain low – only 4% of young cell-owning teens aged 12–17 reported sending sexually explicit photos and 15% receiving one (Lenhart, 2009) – high-profile mainstream media coverage of the few tragic cases keep concerns fresh.

Social Networking

Online social networking is a leading contender for teenagers' time. Rideout et al.'s study (2010) shows that American teenagers spend an average of 22 min a day on SNS, 25% of their overall computer time. Forty percent of young people visit SNS regularly and spend almost an hour (54 min) per day on them. More than half (55%) of online teenagers have profiles on SNS (Lenhart et al., 2007). Lenhart et al.'s study (2007) also shows that most teenagers restrict access to their profiles in some way: 66% set their profile as invisible to the public, nearly half (46%) reveal that they give at least some false information, and most report that they rarely post information on public profiles that would help strangers actually locate them, such as their full name, home phone number, or cell phone number. The study also notes that nearly half (49%) of parents know whether or not their children have an online SNS profile.

Internationally, teenagers are similarly avid about online social networking; however, there are regional differences in terms of how and where teens conduct online social networking, as shown by the world map of social media (Fig. 2) (Cosenza, 2009). This map is based on data collected from Alexa and Google Trends for Web site traffic in December 2009 by Vincenzo Cosenza, an Italian internet analyst and blogger. Cosenza (2009) also summarizes the top three SNS in major countries (Table 2).

There is extensive research on the popularity of Facebook and MySpace in the Western world; however, relatively is known about the development of massive SNS in other regions. For instance, 91.5% of Chinese teenagers consider *QQ*, *Kaixin*, or *Xiaonei* as their major SNS (iResearch, 2009). Nearly every Chinese

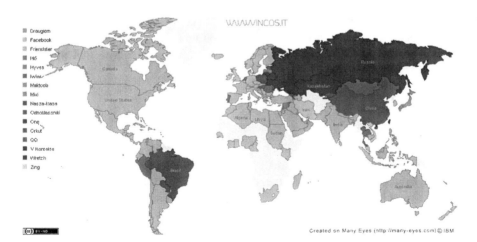

Fig. 2 World map of social networking

Table 2 Top three SNSs

Countries	SNS #1	SNS #2	SNS #3
Australia	Facebook	MySpace	Twitter
Canada	Facebook	MySpace	Flickr
China	QQ	Xiaonei	51
France	Facebook	Skyrock	MySpace
Germany	Facebook	StudiVZ	MySpace
Italy	Facebook	Netlog	Badoo
Russia	V Kontakte	Odnoklassniki	LiveJournal
Spain	Facebook	Tuenti	Fotolog
UK	Facebook	Bebo	MySpace
USA	Facebook	MySpace	Twitter

teenager has an account in *QQ*, the largest social networking platform in China, where one can simultaneously chat in text, audio, and video; play *QQ* games; find friends on *QQ Campus*; and manage profiles in *Qzone*. In South Korea, nearly every young person has a virtual home on *Cyworld*. There is even a new word in South Korea for people who spend too much time in *Cyworld: Cyholics* (Business Week, 2005). A report shows that *Mixi* from Japan hosts 80% of the Japanese social networking market (Market Research Report, 2007). *Orkut*, another popular SNS, is most popular among Indians and Brazilians (Orkut, 2010).

While a majority of teenagers participates in SNS, there are still a sizable number of teenagers who are nonparticipants. Boyd (2007) identifies two types of nonparticipants: *disenfranchised teens* and *conscientious objectors*. According to Boyd's definition, *disenfranchised teens* consist of those without Internet access, those whose parents succeed in banning them from participation, and those who primarily access the Internet through school and other public venues where SNS are blocked. *Conscientious objectors* include politically minded teens protesting against Murdoch's News Corp (the corporate owner of MySpace), obedient teens who respect or agree with their parents' moral or safety concerns, marginalized teens who feel that SNS are for the "cool kids," and those who feel too cool themselves for these sites.

Social Games

Another popular social media activity among young people is social games (Heim, Brandtzæg, Kaare, Endestad, & Torgersen, 2007). Social games are video games driven by turn-taking actions between two or more players (O'Neill, 2008). Social games can be played on standalone game consoles, mobile devices, or SNS, such as Facebook. The most popular social games currently in the USA are Facebook games such as *FarmVille* and *PetVille* (Morrison, 2010), iPhone games such as *Lux Touch* and *Galcon* (Kohler, 2009), and MMOs (massively multiplayer online games) such as *World of Warcraft* (WoW) and *SecondLife*. In China, the top social games in 2009 include *Happy Farm*, *House Buying*, *Parking Wars*, and *Renren Restaurant* (Lukoff, 2009).

Teens spend a significant amount of time playing these online games. According to the Pew Research on teens and video games (2008), nearly all American teens – that is, 97% of 12–17 years olds – play games on computers, the Internet, consoles, or cell phones. Girls (94%) are as likely to play games as boys (99%), but with less frequency and for shorter periods of time. Nearly one-third (31%) of teens are daily gamers. In China, there were 35 million adolescent game-players in 2009, which is 46.1% of the entire social game player population in China, and the game-playing population is increasing at an annual rate of more than 20% (CNNIC, 2009).

MMOs are especially popular among teens in the USA. One in five (21%) teens claims to have played MMOs, and nearly one-third (30%) of boys report that they have had MMO experiences (Lenhart et al., 2008). This is the latest development in a progression of social games from paper-and-pencil fantasy games (e.g., *Dungeons and Dragons*) to text-based multiuser "dungeons" (MUDs) or shared spaces on the Internet to virtual digital worlds online (Steinkuehler & Williams, 2006). In MMOs, players build virtual economies and an entire social world through trading and community involvement activities.

MMOs also provide a virtual reality for young people to study actively and gain more traditional academic skills. The use of MMOs to deliver learning environments is still an emerging area of development and research, but is becoming more popular as games for learning become available. Research is showing that games can be effective learning platforms to teach students about scientific reasoning (Steinkuehler & Duncan, 2008), social sciences (Squire, 2002), literacy (Gee, 2007), foreign languages (Zhao & Lai, 2008), and digital literacy (Steinkuehler, 2008).

Why Do Teens Love Social Media?

Teenagers love social games, live on social networking sites, and text each other constantly. A question on the mind of parents and educators is "Why are social media so attractive and important to them?" Social media fulfill a number of psychological, social, and emotional needs of teenagers, which make them not only extremely popular, but also an essential part of their lives. In this section, we explore how social media tools present teens with opportunities for escape, entertainment, connection, and identity exploration.

Escape

Today's social media provide virtually boundless opportunities to escape from real life. Escapism seems to be a main source of gratification for young Internet users (Leung, 2003). The escapism of social media has both positive and negative consequences. On the one hand, it serves as a coping strategy for adolescents to deal with disturbing family environments, boredom, isolation, discrimination, and depression (Cabiria, 2008; Hwang, Cheong, & Feeley, 2009). Hwang et al. (2009) found that, among adolescents in Taiwan, the higher the rate of depression was for teens, the more likely they were to report engaging in online communication, entertainment, and information searches. Cabiria (2008) argued that virtual worlds provide marginalized gay and lesbian adolescents a place to maintain a sense of personal integrity, community, and well-being. On the other hand, escapism can lead to harmful social relationships, unhealthy lifestyle consequences from a lack of activity, and further depression (Bessière, Pressman, Kiesler, & Kraut, 2010).

Entertainment

Oldenburg (1999) notes that it is essential to the well-being of adults to have a "third space," places like cafés or bookstores that allow people to socialize and expand their world view beyond home and the workplace. Likewise, for adolescents, a "third place" beyond home and school, such as the schoolyard or playground, is important for their social development. However, it is becoming increasingly difficult for children to find this type of space and time to hang-out. Often the rules on behavior for gathering and "hanging out" in public places, including shopping centers, sidewalks, and city parks, have become more restricted with a heightened focus on individual safety (Childress, 2004). Further, children nowadays are often deprived of time to socialize and "hang-out" with their friends because they participate in far more professionally supervised activities during the after-school hours (Gaster, 1991; Afterschool Alliance, 2009).

Under such circumstances, young people look to the virtual "third space" created by SNS, texting, and social games for real-time socialization and communication among old and new friends (Soukup, 2006). In social media, teenagers are able to claim ownership of their own space without having to negotiate with adults. Meanwhile, social media tools provide a place where the users can be temporarily free of their social status and background in real life, which can sometimes be a barrier to their efforts to make friends. Also, tools such as SNS and texting are easy to access, searchable, and archived, thus offering a lasting sense of belonging to a community (Boyd, 2007). These online tools make it possible for adolescents to build a social life that can be harder to establish in their offline, real-world space.

Connections

Social networking enables teenagers to connect with their peers, friends, parents, and strangers. As mentioned earlier, a majority of teenagers play social games to cement their offline friendships and meet new people online (Hundley & Shyles, 2010). In their study on children's perception of social media, Hundley and Shyles (2010) found that users, on average, can have as many as 200 friends on their MySpace "friends" list. They spend time on SNS mainly for the purposes of socialization and entertainment, such as talking with friends, updating their profiles and those of other users, checking their messages, getting in touch with old friends, and meeting new ones, all in one online session.

Mobile phones and text messaging offer the potential of always-on companion-ship and connectedness. As a mobile tool that has the advantage of being private, texting fulfills adolescents' constant curiosity about the lives of their peers and lowers their anxiety about being left out of the loop. As a mother confessed in a *New York Times* blog (Parker-Pope, 2009),

> …[T]exting is how kids stay connected with their peers. It is as ubiquitous as the notes we used to pass in school. For many kids, it's a major part of their social world, and not having it makes them feel like an outcast. At least, that's what my daughter says…I feel her pain.

Indeed, texting helps teens stay in touch in a highly mobile society, including those friends who do not live in close proximity or have moved to another school district, city, state, or country.

In addition, texting has become an important tool for young people to commu-nicate with their parents. A single "hello" text helps to strengthen the bonds of care and connection between parents and children. In a more practical sense, texting and SNS are flexible ways for parents and their teens to monitor each other's where-abouts, stay on top of changing plans, and keep in touch. In addition, texting offers an easy way for parents to reach their adolescents when they are in different time zones because of travel, relocation, or family changes (Chen, 2009).

Exploration

Turkle (1995) views social media as an "identity laboratory" for young people to explore themselves and take on roles that are otherwise inaccessible to them (Gee, 2007). Further, Turkle (1995) has observed that "MUDs [also known as role play-ing games], provide worlds for anonymous social interactions in which one can play a role as close to or as far away from one's 'real self' as one chooses." This is the same case with MMOs, where young players construct their identities or per-sona by taking on distinctive avatar names, profiles, and actions, and by assuming the corresponding social responsibilities and consequences in the virtual world. Meanwhile, cell phones gradually become extensions of young people's bodies and minds (Turkle, 2007) because of all the personal information, including phone numbers, photos, and previous messages, stored in them.

Implications for Students with Special Needs

The multiple uses of social media tools and their impact on the general population certainly apply to students with disabilities. On further examination, these tools hold significant potential for the special needs of population. In this section, we discuss some of the potential benefits of social media, such as removing boundaries to communication and independence, and redefining talents and abilities.

Remove Boundaries

Social media can remove the physical boundaries, such as time and distance, from the academic and social lives of students with disabilities. It is noted that young people with severe disabilities are rarely given the time they need to be able to participate in social interactions (Lindstrand & Brodin, 2004). Online SNS provide channels for special education students to network with friends at any corner of the world around the clock. Learning and communication become mobile with text messaging and other mobile services. The anywhere, anytime mobile learning is further enhanced as a growing number of cell phones (e.g., iPhone), and social media tools (e.g., YouTube) begin to incorporate enhancement functions, such as text-to-speech and zoom for visual impairments, captions for hearing impairments, and voice control for motor skill impairment.

The learning opportunities for students with disabilities outside the classroom become enriched with the ever-increasing user-generated contents on online sites such as Facebook and YouTube, as well as mobile phone applications. For example, Sailers (2009) discusses the proliferation of iPhone applications that are useful for special education students, such as literacy apps (e.g., *ABC PocketPhonics*, *See Read Say*, *iWrite Words*), math apps (e.g., *Cute Math*, *Freddy Fraction*, *Graphing Calculator*), organization apps (e.g., *Awesome Note*, *BehaviorTrackerPro*), music apps (e.g., *Bloom*, *TonePad*), art and game apps (e.g., *ColorSplash*, *Preschool Adventure*), and communication apps (e.g., *ABA Flashcards*, *ArtickPix*, *Proloquo2Go*). The common feature of these apps is that they are easy to use, low cost, readily available, and accessible.

The second potential benefit of these social media tools is the reduction in social and emotional distance between student with disabilities, their peers, teachers, and the rest of the world. Social media offer a psychologically safe space that enables social interactions via multiple channels. The anonymity of social media may make students with disabilities more open to socialize with others and more willing to ask for help online than in face-to-face situations. Online SNS designed specifically for students with learning and intellectual disabilities, such as Special Friends Online (http://www.specialfriendsonline.com), help special education students and their caretakers connect with one another.

There is growing evidence indicating that computer-based collaboration improves the peer acceptance of children with ADHD, who are often subject to peer rejection and social isolation. A case study of an adolescent with ADHD in Singapore shows that computer-based collaborative group work improved the boy's peer acceptance among his classmates (Tan & Cheung, 2006). An earlier study by Repman (1993) suggests that computer collaborative work not only enhances the students' self-esteem, but also provides a third-party focus that facilitates children with ADHD to develop successful peer group participation. The evidence suggests the merits of integrating SNS, text messaging, and social games in the design of collaborative learning experiences for encouraging positive cooperation between students with special needs and their peers with or without special needs.

Young people with physical deficits benefit socially from social media as well. A recent study on children with an autism spectrum disorder (ASD) indicates that a collaborative virtual learning environment has significant positive effects on the social competence and social interaction of children with an ASD (Cheng & Ye, 2009). A child with high-functioning autism, for instance, may have a close to normal IQ and function effectively in literal contexts, but have difficulty using language in a social context (Gal et al., 2009). Online social networking or text messaging may facilitate these children to sustain their social interaction by avoiding the awkwardness of face-to-face social situations. These tools allow the users to express themselves at their own pace, through their preferred medium, and in their private space, with fewer expectations of immediate social and emotional feedback. Social games such as MMOs may be employed to design virtual social learning environments for children with autism and other conditions.

Some educators and parents have expressed concern that technology may worsen the issue of isolation by distracting children with disabilities from playing with their current school or neighborhood friends (Brodin & Lindstrand, 2004). However, research on general education college students shows that online SNS such as Facebook helps students both make new friends and bond with existing friends (Ellison, Steinfield, & Lampe, 2007). A similar phenomenon may emerge among special education students as well, although that needs to be confirmed with further empirical research.

As a critical tool and resource for caregivers, social media can be used for many purposes including promoting safe independence, reinforcing bonds, and creating support networks. The online SNS (such as Special Friends Online, mentioned earlier), together with assistive tools online, can significantly enhance the communication between caregivers and young people with disabilities. Social games, played online or on cell phones, offer an alternative and easy way for caregivers to bond with young people with disabilities.

Live update sites, such as Facebook, MySpace, Twitter, and FourSquare, and text messaging can provide information about a young person's whereabouts without the overbearing constant presence by a caregiver. These applications are being used not only by parents to track their children's activities, but can also be used to deliver real-time mentoring by job coaches or counselors for young people who may need reminders and prompts as they begin employment.

Other social networking activities offer flexible and expansive online communities for parents and caregivers to bond with others by exchanging information on treatments and medications, swapping tips, and sharing everyday joys and challenges. Numerous studies illustrate the power of social media as an integral tool for communication among parents, teachers, doctors, and other professionals. Further, there are numerous examples of the use of social media as powerful tools for parents and caretakers to advocate for their children and raise societal awareness of students with learning, intellectual, and physical difficulties.

Redefine Talents

Social media tools play a vital role in redefining talents for students with disabilities. As the saying goes, "when one door closes, another opens." This might be the case for young people with disabilities. Life stories of both prominent scientists and ordinary people show that a deficit in one ability can be compensated by special talents in other areas. John Nash, the well-known subject of the 2001 Hollywood movie, *A Beautiful Mind*, is a mathematical genius and Nobel Prize winner who has battled schizophrenia throughout his life. Molecular biologist Carol Greider won the 2009 Nobel Prize for Medicine, after years of struggling with dyslexia. In an interview with the *New York Times*, Greider noted that since she was aware of her difficulty with spelling, she focused on ways to compensate, such as memorizing words and objects with photographic aids, which boosted her initial interest in chemistry and later achievement in telomeres (Dreifus, 2009). Greider confessed that she did poorly on standardized tests in schools, and her GRE scores fell short of her peers, resulting in acceptance from only two of the ten universities to which she had applied for graduate studies. However, Greider also noted that "dyslexia is a different way of viewing the world, and sometimes, it's an advantage" (Minkove, 2009).

Nevertheless, only a relatively small percentage of people with special needs are able to have their special talents honed and acknowledged. While not every student with disabilities demonstrates special skills, many of them do have remarkable talents that are often ignored or mislabeled. An important reason is that the current assessment system for disability is not designed in a way to appreciate, encourage, and nurture the special talents of students with special needs.

Theories such as multiple intelligences pose serious challenges to the legitimacy of the existing intelligence assessment model that prioritizes verbal and math skills over other talents (Gardner, 1999; Gardner & Hatch, 1989). Educators debate over how to define normality, ability, and talents, and what they should and can be in the twenty-first century (Zhao, 2009). As Zhao suggests that the parameters of abilities and talents are bound to change in an era where currently esteemed careers and economic sectors may not exist in 10–20 years. Disability researchers point to the fact that *all* people with disabilities have the potential to develop special skills, and stress that the exposure to options and opportunities plays a large part in determining the life path of an individual (Happé & Frith, 2009).

Because they offer an environment in which to recognize, nurture, and assess the special talents of disabled students, social media tools need to become an integral part of the educational system. Social media offer multiple channels of expression (i.e., visual, audio, textual, behavioral, or combined) that allow the talents of all students to emerge. Lee Abramson, a Michigan resident, has amyotrophic lateral sclerosis, or ALS, a terminal disease that severely impairs the patient's motor skills and even consciousness (Bertsos, 2009). Nevertheless, the disease did not stop him from becoming an inspiring songwriter online. Abramson uses YouTube and

MySpace and other assistive tools to write and broadcast his own music, which has won him accolades and access to audiences all over the world.

As discussed earlier, social networks are democratic, innovative, and often, grassroots in nature, allowing for the co-existence of different talents. There are numerous online communities, such as Artists and Autism on Facebook, and a YouTube video that shares the story of an artist with autism has attracted more than 230,000 hits. In a way, social media offers a sense of belonging, social identification, and self-esteem, all of which can be difficult to find in ordinary life, but which are indispensable to the well-being and growth of people with disabilities. Connecting with a real audience online becomes a strong motivator for students with disabilities to develop their special talents with greater intensity.

Conclusion

There is little doubt that social media have become a dominant force in the life of today's youth. As a relatively new phenomenon, there is still much to learn about their ultimate impact on students. However, it is clear that social media and networking tools meet a variety of needs for all youth and offer powerful potential for youth with disabilities.

To summarize, the power of social media for students with disabilities lies in three areas. First, it removes physical distances and can significantly expand the living space of youth who otherwise are confined by their disabilities. With social media, they can now participate in activities that may be taking place thousands of miles away. Furthermore, with the distance factor removed, they can make friends with those with similar disabilities and form a large social network with people in similar situations, but who might otherwise not be accessible. Second, social media enable parents, teachers, and other caregivers of special need students to form communities of their own to provide emotional and social support as well as to share treatment and coping strategies. Lastly, social media provide multiple ways for students to participate in a variety of activities. Students with disabilities in one area can use technology to exploit their strengths in others.

The full potential of social media for students with disabilities has yet to be explored. To take advantage of these innovative technologies, we need to prepare educators, parents, school administrators, and other caregivers to be proficient in social media and understand the potential of these tools for students with disabilities. Moreover, schools and other education agencies for students with disabilities need to be proactive, rather than over-protective. Schools need to help students with disabilities gain access to social media and educate them about the uses as well as potential dangers. Finally, more research needs to be conducted on the effects and best practices of social media tools for students with disabilities to better support them and provide opportunities to maximize their academic and personal potential.

References

Afterschool Alliance. (2009). *America after 3 PM*. Retrieved from http://www.afterschoolalliance. org/AA3_Full_Report.pdf.

Ambrogi, S. (2009). "Sexting" craze on the rise among British children. *Reuters*. Retrieved from http://www.reuters.com/article/idUSTRE5733SG20090804.

Bertsos, C. (2009, September 2). Local man uses music to combat disease. *The State News*.

Bessière, K., Pressman, S., Kiesler, S., & Kraut, R. (2010). Effects of Internet use on health and depression: A longitudinal study. *Journal of Medical Internet Research, 12*(1), e6.

Boyd, D. (2007). Why youth (heart) social network sites: The role of networked publics in teenage social life. In D. Buckingham (Ed.), *MacArthur Foundation series on digital learning – Youth, identity, and digital media* (pp. 119–142). Cambridge, MA: MIT Press.

Brodin, J., & Lindstrand, P. (2004). Are computers the solution to support development in children in need of special support? *Technology and Disabilities, 16*(3), 137–145.

Business Week. (2005, September 26). E-Society: My world is cyworld. *Business Week*.

Cabiria, J. (2008). Virtual world and real world permeability: Transference of positive benefits for marginalized gay and lesbian populations. *Journal of Virtual Worlds Research, 1*(1), 1–13.

Cavazza, F. (2009). *Social media landscape redux*. Retrieved from http://www.fredcavazza. net/2009/04/10/social-media-landscape-redux/.

Chen, P. (2009, November 5). Texting as a health tool for teenagers. *New York Times*.

Cheng, Y., & Ye, J. (2009). Exploring the social competence of students with autism spectrum conditions in a collaborative virtual learning environment – The pilot study. *Computers & Education, 54*(4), 1068–1077.

Childress, H. (2004). Teenagers, territory and the appropriation of space. *Childhood, 11*(2), 195–205.

CNNIC. (2009). *2009 Chinese online game market research report*. Retrieved from http://www. cnnic.net.cn/uploadfiles/pdf/2009/11/24/110832.pdf.

Cosenza, V. (2009). *World map of social networks*. Retrieved from http://www.vincos.it/world-map-of-social-networks/.

Dreifus, C. (2009, October 12). A conversation with Carol W. Greider on winning a Nobel Prize in science. *New York Times*.

Ellison, N. B., Steinfield, C., & Lampe, C. (2007). The benefits of Facebook "friends": Social capital and college students' use of online social network sites. *Journal of Computer-Mediated Communication, 12*(4). Retrieved from http://jcmc.indiana.edu/vol12/issue14/ellison.html.

Entner, R. (2010). *Under-aged texting: Usage and actual cost*. Retrieved from http://blog.nielsen. com/nielsenwire/online_mobile/under-aged-texting-usage-and-actual-cost/.

Gal, E., Bauminger, N., Goren-Bar, D., Pianesi, F., Stock, O., Zancanaro, M., et al. (2009). Enhancing social communication of children with high-functioning autism through a co-located interface. *AI & Society, 24*(1), 75–84.

Gardner, H. (1999). *The disciplined mind: Beyond facts and standardized tests, The K-12 education that every child deserves*. New York: Simon and Schuster (and New York: Penguin Putnam).

Gardner, H., & Hatch, T. (1989). Multiple intelligences go to school: Educational implications of the theory of multiple intelligences. *Educational Researcher, 18*(8), 4–9.

Gaster, S. (1991). Urban children's access to their neighborhood: Changes over three generations. *Environment and Behavior, 23*(1), 70–85.

Gee, J. P. (2007). *What video games have to teach us about learning and literacy*. New York: Macmillan.

GSMA & NTT Docomo. (2009). Children's use of mobile phones: An international comparison. Retrieved from http://www.gsmworld.com/documents/Final_report.pdf.

Happé, F., & Frith, U. (2009). The beautiful otherness of the autistic mind. *Philosophical Transactions of the Royal Society B, 364*, 1345–1350.

Heim, J., Brandtzæg, P. B., Kaare, B. H., Endestad, T., & Torgersen, L. (2007). Children's usage of media technologies and psychosocial factors. *New Media Society, 9*(3), 425–454.

Hundley, H. L., & Shyles, L. (2010). U.S. teenagers' perceptions and awareness of digital technology: A focus group approach. *New Media Society*, doi:10.1177/1461444809342558.

Hwang, J. M., Cheong, P. H., & Feeley, T. H. (2009). Being young and feeling blue in Taiwan: Examining adolescent depressive mood and online and offline activities. *New Media Society, 11*(7), 1101–1121.

iResearch. (2009). *2009 iResearch report on Chinese teenagers' behavior on the Internet.* Retrieved from http://report.iresearch.cn/1270.html.

Kaplan, A., & Haenlein, M. (2010). Users of the world, unite! The challenges and opportunities of social media. *Business Horizons, 53*(1), 59–68.

Kohler, C. (2009). Top 10 iPhone games, as voted by Wired.com readers. *Wired.*

Lenhart, A. (2009). *Teens and sexting: How and why minor teens are sending sexually suggestive nude or nearly nude images via text messaging.* Washington, DC: Pew Internet & American Life Project.

Lenhart, A., Kahne, J., Middaugh, E., Macgill, A., Evans, C., & Vitak, J. (2008). *Teens, video games and civics.* Washington, DC: Pew Internet & American Life Project.

Lenhart, A., Madden, M., Macgill, A., & Smith, A. (2007). *Teens and social media.* Washington, DC: Pew Internet & American Life Project.

Leung, L. (2003). Impacts of Net-generation attributes, seductive properties of the Internet, and gratifications-obtained on Internet use. *Telematics and Informatics, 20*(2), 107–129.

Lindstrand, P., & Brodin, J. (2004). Parents and children view ICT. *Technology and Disabilities, 16*(3), 179–183.

Lukoff, K. (2009). Top 10 social games in China. *The Next Web.com.* Retrieved from http://thenextweb.com/asia/2009/12/15/top-10-social-games-china/.

Lyman, P., Billings, A., Ellinger, S., Finn, M., & Perkel, D. (2005). *Literature review: Kids' informal learning and digital-mediated experiences.* White paper for MacArthur Foundation.

Market Research Report. (2007). *Mixi: A case study of Japan's most successful social networking service.* Infinita.

Mayfield, A. (2008). *What is social media? (V.1.4).* Retrieved from http://www.icrossing.co.uk/.../What_is_Social_Media_iCrossing_ebook.pdf.

McLuhan, M., & Gordon, W. T. (2003). *Understanding media: the extensions of man.* Corte Madera, CA: Gingko Press.

MDA. (2010). *UK sends 11 million text messages an hour.* Retrieved from http://www.themda.org/mda-press-releases/the-q4-2009-uk-mobile-trends-report.php.

Ministry of Industry and Information Technology. (2006). *About the charge of telephone in Beijing.* Retrieved April 16, 2010, from http://www.miit.gov.cn/n11293472/n11293832/n11294327/n11303938/11641157.html.

Minkove, J. F. (2009). *Prized curiosity. Dome: A publication for the Johns Hopkins Medicine Family.* Retrieved from http://www.hopkinsmedicine.org/dome/1109/headliners1.cfm.

Morrison, C. (2010). *Zynga takes the top three on this week's list of top Facebook gainers by DAU.* Retrieved from http://www.insidesocialgames.com/2010/03/31/zynga-takes-the-top-three-on-this-weeks-list-of-top-facebook-gainers-by-dau/.

Mundy, L. (2010, March 28). In Japan, teenage cellphone culture makes real connections. *The Washington Post.*

Naish, J. (2009). Mobile phones for children: A boon or a peril? *Timesonline.* Retrieved from http://women.timesonline.co.uk/tol/life_and_style/women/families/article6556283.ece.

O'Neill, N. (2008). What exactly are social games? *Social Times.* Retrieved from http://www.socialtimes.com/2008/07/social-games/.

Oldenburg, R. (1999). *The great good place.* New York: Marlowe & Company.

Orkut. (2010). *Orkut demographics.* Retrieved from http://www.orkut.co.in/MembersAll.aspx.

Parker-Pope, T. (2009). *When Dad banned text messaging.* Retrieved from http://well.blogs.nytimes.com/2009/03/30/when-dad-banned-text-messaging/.

Repman, J. (1993). Collaborative, computer-based learning: cognitive and avective outcomes. *Journal of Educational Computing Research, 9*, 149–173.

Rideout, C. J., Foehr, U. G., & Roberts, D. F. (2010). *Generation M²: Media in the lives of 8- to 18-year-olds (A Kaiser Family Foundation study).* Menlo Park, CA: Henry J. Kaiser Family Foundation.

Sailers, E. (2009). *iPhone and iPod touch apps for (special) education*. Retrieved from http://www.mpf.org/iPhone%20and%20iPod%20apps%20for%20sp.pdf.

Soukup, C. (2006). Computer-mediated communication as a virtual third place: Building Oldenburg's great good places on the world wide web. *New Media Society, 8*(3), 421–440.

Squire, K. D. (2002). Rethinking the role of games in education. *Game Studies, 2*(1). Retrieved Feburary 07, 2011, from http://www.gamestudies.org/0102/squire/

Steinkuehler, C. (2008). Cognition and literacy in massively multiplayer online games. In J. Coiro, M. Knobel, C. Lankshear, & D. Leu (Eds.), *Handbook of research on new literacies* (pp. 611–634). Mahwah, NJ: Erlbaum.

Steinkuehler, C., & Duncan, S. C. (2008, August). Informal scientific reasoning in online game forums. Presented at the annual meeting of the American Psychological Association, Boston, MA.

Steinkuehler, C., & Williams, D. (2006). Where everybody knows your (screen) name: Online games as "third places". *Journal of Computer-Mediated Communication, 11*(4), 885–909.

Tan, T. S., & Cheung, W. S. (2006). Effects of computer collaborative group work on peer acceptance of a junior pupil with attention deficit hyperactivity disorder (ADHD). *Computers & Education, 50*(3), 725–741.

Thurlow, C., & Brown, A. (2002). Generation txt? The sociolinguistics of young people's text-messaging. *Discourse Analysis Online, 1*(1). Retrieved Feburary 07, 2011, from http://faculty.washington.edu/thurlow/papers/Thurlow(2003)-DAOL.pdf

Turkle, S. (1995). *Life on the screen*. New York: Simon & Schuster.

Turkle, S. (2007). *Evocative objects*. Cambridge, MA: MIT Press.

Zhao, Y. (2009). *Catching up or keeping the lead: American education in the age of globalization*. Alexandria, VA: ASCD.

Zhao, Y., & Lai, C. (2008). Massively multi-player online role playing games (MMORPGS) and foreign language education. In R. Ferdig (Ed.), *Handbook of research on effective electronic gaming in education*. New York: IDEA Group.

Exergames Get Kids Moving

Stephen Yang and John Foley

The realization that children's physical activity is of national concern was highlighted in First Lady Michelle Obama's launch of the Let's Move campaign. "The physical and emotional health of an entire generation and the economic health and security of our nation is at stake. This isn't the kind of problem that can be solved overnight, but with everyone working together, it can be solved. So, let's move!" she said at the launch ceremony (2010). Getting children *moving* can be surprisingly difficult, but remarkably beneficial to a number of health indicators. The Let's Move campaign draws attention to the relationship between lifestyle choices and health.

The 2007–2008 National Health and Nutrition Examination Survey found that 34.79% of U.S. school-aged youth were overweight or at risk of being overweight (Ogden, Carroll, Curtin, Lamb, & Flegal, 2010). There are many factors that contribute to this crisis. Poor eating habits receive the greatest amount of attention, but the amount of time spent doing sedentary activities is also a concern. The average 8- to 18-year-old spends nearly 8 h with various forms of media including watching television, using computers, and playing video games (Rideout, Foehr, & Roberts, 2010). Eighty-seven percent of U.S. youngsters between the ages of 8 and 18 have a video game console at home and half of them have a video game console in their bedroom (Rideout et al., 2010; Roberts, Foehr, & Rideout, 2005). Clearly children and adolescents love playing video games but, until recently, many educators did not consider video games to be healthful or educational.

A paradigm shift is underway, fueled by a group of video games – and video game controllers that allow players to physically interact with the game – called exergames or active games. Because exergames require much more physical activity than the traditional games and can offer more peer interaction, these games are becoming a tool to engage students physically, psychologically, and socially.

This chapter explores how active gaming or exergaming can assist individuals with disabilities to become more active, gain motor skills, and enjoy a more inclusive gaming experience. The relationship between motor skills and healthy weight is

S. Yang (✉)
SUNY-Cortland, Cortland, NY, USA
e-mail: stephen.yang@cortland.edu

T. Gray and H. Silver-Pacuilla (eds.), *Breakthrough Teaching and Learning:*
How Educational and Assistive Technologies are Driving Innovation,
DOI 10.1007/978-1-4419-7768-7_6, © Springer Science+Business Media, LLC 2011

discussed first as a backdrop to the importance of physical activity and of including children with disabilities in physical education programs. The next section explores exergames and the emerging research base that indicates potential physical as well as psychological benefits. Several commercially available games are described, along with the research investigating their impacts and suggestions for adapting them for students with disabilities. Finally, the future of the exergame genre is considered as well as how educational leaders can advocate for the inclusion of exergames as part of a physical education program.

The Importance of Physical Activity

There is a growing body of evidence demonstrating the importance of mastering motor skills – such as running, jumping, balancing, and throwing – on physical activity and obesity. In general, these skills are found to be lower or less developed for children with disabilities (Drowatzky & Geiger, 1993). Tilinger and Lejcarova (2003) suggest that poor performance in cardiovascular fitness may be the product of low motor skills. Other work has also provided evidence to indicate that children who are less physically active tend to have lower motor skills (Kim, Matsuura, Tanaka, & Inagaki, 1993; Rosa, Rodriguez, & Marquez, 1996). As one would expect, adolescents who participate in greater amounts of organized physical activity have been shown to have better motor skills (Okely, Booth, & Patterson, 2001). It has also been shown that children who scored poorly on motor development tests had a higher propensity to be overweight (Graf et al., 2004).

Developing fundamental motor skills may directly and indirectly affect health body mass, or body fatness, as seen in Fig. 1 (Foley, Harvey, Chun, & Kim, 2008). This diagram, summarizing the findings of research conducted with adolescences with intellectual disabilities, indicates that one's motor skills could directly influences one's fitness and that some of that improvement attributable to the motor skill can also be attributed to changes in body fatness. Simply stated, the more easily your body moves in the physical environment, the easier or more likely it is to maintain a healthy level of fitness and thereby, weight. (Learn more about healthy weight, body mass index (BMI), and body fatness at http://www.cdc.gov/healthyweight/assessing/bmi/childrens_bmi/about_childrens_bmi.html.) Since youth with disabilities are at greater risk of having poor motor skills and unhealthy weight, increased awareness in fundamental motor skills along with physical activity may help attenuate the high obesity levels.

The current physical activity guidelines for youth are for 60 min of moderate to vigorous activity a day, based on the Physical Activity Guidelines Advisory Committee Report (U.S. Department of Health and Human Services, 2008). These guidelines cite numerous studies to demonstrate that the benefits of exercise may use the same thresholds for both individuals with and without disabilities. Evidence suggests that increased physical activity is associated with improvement of mental health outcomes, decreased body fatness, increased functional independence, and greater muscular strength.

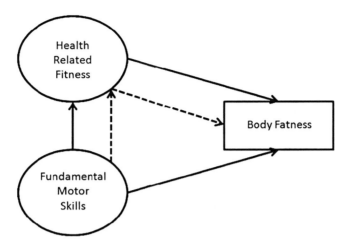

Fig. 1 A model of the relationship of body fatness, health-related fitness, and fundamental motor skills; adapted from Foley et al. (2008)

As a group, individuals with physical and/or developmental disabilities comprise the largest minority group in the USA (Olkin, 1999). Fully 78% of all U.S. citizens have some type of disability, and of those, 87% are at increased risk of related negative health outcomes (U.S. Department of Health and Human Services, 2005). Increased physical activity can prevent or mitigate many of these negative outcomes, such as diabetes, unhealthy weight, and heart disease.

However, individuals with disabilities tend to be less physically active than individuals without disabilities. Of the adult population with disabilities, over 65% engage in *no* leisure-time physical activity, compared to less than 25% of the adult population without disabilities (Healthy People 2010, 2004). While research exists investigating the daily physical activity levels of children in the general population, little work has been done to examine the physical activity levels of children with disabilities (Fernhall & Unnithan, 2002).

When Healthy People 2010 was released in 2004, it was a collective effort between federal agencies to establish national health objectives that were identified as the most significant threat to public health. One of the objectives was to decrease the health disparities that exist between individuals with and without disabilities. To help reduce this disparity, a goal was set to increase the percentage of individuals with disabilities engaged in daily moderate to vigorous physical activity. Data from the CDC in Fig. 2 indicate that, to date, this goal has not been met.

The Role of Physical Education in Schools

Participation in physical education (PE) on a regular basis for all children has been linked to multiple positive outcomes. Participation in PE in the schools may be effective in reducing the onset of obesity in elementary school-aged children

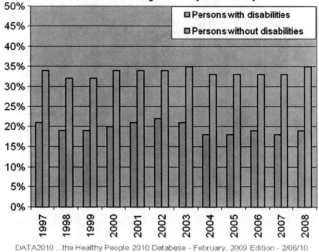

Fig. 2 Disparity in physical activity

(Datar, Sturm, & Magnabosco, 2004). In addition, a critical review of the research by the CDC (2010) confirmed that these benefits carry over to academic achievement as well, with time spent in physical activity is correlated with higher academic functioning in youth. Further, this report supported the notion that regular physical activity through PE class or recess is associated with increased concentration and on-tasked behavior.

PE or adapted physical education is the optimal learning environment for improvement in motor skills and increased physical activity for youth with disabilities. This is supported by federal legislation, specifically the Individuals with Disabilities Education Act (IDEA) 2004, which identified adapted physical education as a direct service of special education. (See Text Box 1 for the definition of physical education under the law.)

Adapted physical education is tailored to the unique needs of individual students. Its role as an educational service is to assist students in achieving their true potential in the physical domains. As students move into adolescence, it is imperative that students make a connection between lifelong fitness and active leisure activities and available resources in the community. It is important to note that adapted physical education is mandated as a direct service under IDEA law, whereas physical therapy and occupational therapy are listed as related services.

Among schools in the USA that serve students with disabilities, about 85% of those students participate in the regular PE curriculum and about 38% participate in both regular and adapted PE (Burgeson, Wechsler, Brener, Young, & Spain, 2001). It is the position of the American Alliance for Health, Physical Education,

Recreation, and Dance that students with disabilities be included to the fullest extent in the general physical education curriculum (American Association for Active Lifestyles and Fitness, 2004).

Box 1 The Definition of Physical Education as Defined by Federal Law

Physical education means

1. The development of

   (a) Physical and motor fitness
   (b) Fundamental motor skills and patterns
   (c) Skills in aquatics, dance, and individual and group games and sports (including intramural and lifetime sports)

2. Includes special physical education, adapted physical education, movement education, and motor development.

   From IDEA – Building the legacy at http://idea.ed.gov/explore/view/ p/%-2Croot%2Cregs%2C300%2CA%2C300%252E39%2Cb%2C2%2C

The opening chapter (Gray, Silver-Pacuilla, Brann, Overton, & Reynolds, this volume) references the growing number of children with special health care needs who require health and related services beyond the routine for ongoing physical, emotional, behavioral, or developmental conditions. An estimated 10.2 million children have such needs (U.S. Department of Health and Human Services, 2008), a number which reflects 13–20% of all children and adolescents (Bethell, Read, Blumberg, & Newacheck, 2008; Mulye et al., 2009). Children with these conditions may or may not be receiving special education services, clinical therapy, or assistive technology devices or services. Some of the fastest growing childhood special health conditions include autism, attention disorders, obesity, diabetes, and asthma. Children with these conditions often have limited opportunities to participate in traditional sports and/or physical education without some accommodations and modifications.

Enter Exergames

Children and adolescents love to play video games; in fact they make up 25% of all computer and video game players (Entertainment Software Association, 2009). As cited above, gaming at home is becoming an everyday occurrence for most U.S. children (Rideout et al., 2010). Besides playing video games on game consoles and handheld devices, youngsters also play video games on their home computers and almost all (91%) who have computers at home use them to play video games (U.S. Department of Education, 2003).

Traditionally, video games have been played by gamers sitting in front of a screen by pushing buttons or moving a joystick. Many health experts feel video games contribute to the childhood and adolescent obesity epidemic; however, the niche of video games and controllers that require the player to move their body or body parts in order to play the game, called exergames or active games, is growing (Yang, Smith, & Graham, 2008). While many physical educators and parents would prefer to see youngsters obtaining their physical activity through sports, it seems increasingly clear that for youngsters today, exergames may be a popular alternative to sports like soccer and football.

Exergames require the player to move parts of the body or the entire body to play. In essence, the player becomes the character in the video game in a form of augmented reality (Matysczok, Radkowski, & Berssenbruegge, 2004; Ohshima, Satoh, Yamamoto, & Tamura, 1998). In order to play these games, players must be physically active and moving.

Exergames have the advantage of being played in a more climate-controlled environment for those with asthma and allergies; at a controlled pace, intensity, and duration for those who are building their stamina; and on a controlled and predictable surface for those with vision and motor impairments. If these games can be as motivating to play as traditional video games, but with additional physical benefits, we should continue to explore whether or not some of these games are suitable for students of varying abilities.

An Emerging Research Base

While exergames have been used by some professionals, such as physical therapists, for rehabilitation activities (Flynn, Palma, & Bender, 2007), and as a low intensity activity for the elderly (Arciero et al., 2009; Robusto & Nichols, 2010), the research base, especially for individuals with disabilities, is still new. The field got a boost in 2008 when the Robert Wood Johnson Foundation's (RWJF) Pioneer Portfolio dedicated $8.25 million to support researchers investigating the potential health benefits from playing games such as exergames. With this newly created Health Games Research program (http://healthgamesresearch.org), RWJF is the first large foundation to recognize the potential role exergames may play in getting people to be more active and healthy.

This effort builds upon RWJF's investment in games as learning environments. This investment began with their 2005 backing of the Serious Games Initiative, which in turn supports several initiatives including Games for Change (http://www.gamesforchange.org) and Games for Health (http://www.gamesforhealth.org). Within the Games for Health initiative, separate tracks dedicated to exergaming and game accessibility are supported, culminating in an annual international conference. The Game Accessibility strand has grown each year, and has become a professional network of developers, researchers, and advocates hosted year-round by the Able Gamers advocacy group (http://www.ablegamers.com). (See the appended resource list for more advocacy groups.)

Research into how exergames provide adapted physical activity for children with disabilities or special health care needs indicates real potential for health benefits as well as important parallel benefits including improvement in cognitive skills, mobility and range of motion skills, and engagement.

Cognitive skills. Middle-school students with Attention-Deficit/Hyperactivity Disorder (ADHD) played a full-body dance game, *Dance Dance Revolution* (*DDR*), at school. On pre- and posttests of reading skills, students who played the game made statistically significant gains on a few key subskills, with those students who engaged in more play sessions showing stronger gains. Researchers hypothesize that attention and short-term memory may be boosted by the intense concentration required to step to the rhythm and follow directions that scroll quickly across the screen during game play (McGraw, Burdette, & Chadwick, 2005). In another pilot study of a dance game, the *iDANCE* system, used for 12 weeks (10 min daily), students' math and language scores increased 6–8% each (Positive Gaming AB, 2010).

Mobility and range of motion skills. Adolescents with mobility impairments due to spina bifida which prevented them from participating in sports benefited from playing a *GameCycle* video game with their arms. This game combines the crank mechanism from a hand cycle with a commercially available game system (GameCube; Nintendo Co., Ltd, Kyoto, Japan) to play a car racing game (*Need for Speed II*; EA Games, Redwood City, CA). The user cranks the handles to control the speed of the car in the video game. Direction is controlled by tilting the crank handles, similar to steering a hand cycle. The crank resistance can be altered to increase the work required, and crank speed can be calibrated to increase the aerobic effort. Seven out of eight of the participants were able to achieve an intensity level that gave them aerobic exercise in their sessions three times a week. Moreover, the participants reported that they enjoyed the exercise and were motivated to play (Widman, McDonald, & Abresch, 2006).

Children with cerebral palsy (CP) have been shown to improve range of motion and strength from adapted video and exergames. In one study, three adolescents with CP which resulted in little use of one hand were given access to teletherapy rehabilitation delivered through video games. Through a specially designed glove, they controlled a hand-shaped avatar on the screen, thus encouraging an increased use of the hands and fingers. The participants improved in range of motion, coordination, and in two of the three participants, increased bone density of the impacted arm. The games and game play were monitored remotely at a clinic while the adolescents played the games at their homes (Golomb et al., 2010). Deutsch and colleagues (2008) worked with an adolescent with CP who played full-body games with the Wii. Their work over the summer (11 sessions) with the student resulted in improvements in postural control, visual-perceptual processing, and functional mobility. His game therapy occurred with other nondisabled peers, which was listed as a real positive socialization benefit for the individual. Jannink et al. (2008) worked with ten children with CP to increase motor skills and strength in their arms by playing exergames at moderate intensity with the EyeToy. Arm function was improved in the 6-week intervention and the children reported high levels of satisfaction and motivation with the exergame training.

Engagement. Despite what is known about exergames' impact physiologically, less is known about their psychological impacts. A recent study analyzed the differences between a standardized five-stage treadmill fitness test and running at the same cadence while playing *Wii Fit Free Run* (*FFR*) (Abbott, McElroy, & Ruocco, 2009). The researchers found nonsignificant differences in the overall average heart rate and energy expenditure but a significant difference in *perceived* level of exertion. The college-aged students performed the two activities at about the same rate, but somehow they were sufficiently distracted from the intensity or perhaps even enjoyed playing *FFR* more than running on the treadmill. This finding is not surprising given the distracting and immersive effects of playing games. This is supported by Warburton's two studies on playing on a *GameBike* (Source Distributors) hooked to a PS2 (Warburton et al., 2007, 2009). Participants enjoyed the *GameBike* more despite working out harder (2007); and in a second study, participants exercising at a higher work capacity reported similar levels of perceived exertion compared to a control group (2009). Adolescents with visual impairments reported a high level of enjoyment while playing *DDR*, EyeToy *Kinetic*, and Wii *Boxing* at a summer camp (Boffoli & Foley, 2010).

Adapting Exergames

Children with disabilities enjoy playing video games as much as their nondisabled peers and even 5 years ago were playing an average of 15–30 min a day, sometimes on multiple game consoles (Lesher & Monasterio, 2004). However, each console, controller, and game has different levels of accessibility and that can be a real source of frustration for game players that require special modifications in order to play (Bierre, 2005). Luckily, there is a growing community of game developers, console and control makers, and advocates who are continuing to advocate for the needs of the accessible gamer.

Accessibility of video and exergames is critical for individuals with disabilities. Given the complexity of the games, there are a number of mismatches that can occur and must be overcome for the gamer to participate fully. Table 1 presents an overview of the challenges individuals with disabilities may face (Bierre, 2005; Kalapanidas et al., 2009).

Following are overviews of commercially available and affordable exergames, such as *DDR*, EyeToy, XaviX *Tennis*, Nintendo Wii, and *Guitar Hero*. Each is described below for their potential benefit, related research on health benefits, and how they can be adapted to meet a number of student needs.

DDR is a dance simulation that is probably the most well-known exergame, as it has been around the longest and is available on all game platforms and arcade machines. It draws on popular music and it gets players moving together. The gameplay (how the game is played) is all about thinking, doing, and decision making (Prensky, 2001) which is compelling and fun. *DDR* requires players to step on a dance pad to the beat and rhythm of various types of popular, child- and teen-oriented

Table 1 Types of disability and potential impact on game play (adapted from Bierre, 2005; Kalapanidas et al., 2009)

Impairment or disability	Potential impact on game play
Auditory – deaf or hard of hearing	• Could prevent gamer from following cut scenes that may contain plot information • Could prevent gamer from receiving game cues such as footsteps or other sounds
Visual – blindness, low vision, or color blindness	• Color schemes may make it difficult for the color blind to receive game cues • Small objects on the screen may not be visible to those with low vision • Visually based games will not be accessible to the blind
Mobility	• Games that do not support alterative input devices may be inaccessible • A lack of configurable difficulty levels could prevent gamers from being able to set a usable level
Psychological	• Game scenes might create or trigger symptoms of psychological nature • The lack of adaptable or customizable game content could prevent gamers from achieving therapeutic goals • Certain game types might be unsuitable for certain psychological disorders
Cognitive	• Lack of a tutorial mode could be a problem • A large printed manual may be ineffective for gamers with ADD or ADHD • Games that require a lot of micromanagement will be difficult for those with memory loss

music as arrows scroll up the monitor. Alternately, *DDR* can be played on other input devices such as a typical hand controller, hand pad, finger pad, or a specially adapted hand controller, such as the desktop controller in Fig. 3. Players receive points and cheers when they step in time (in sync) with the flashing arrows.

DDR can be a physical workout of low or moderate intensity (Bailey, Marcelus, Lujares, Kennard, & McInnis, 2008; Chin A Paw, Jacobs, Vaessena, Titzeb, & Mechelen 2008; Graf, Pratt, Hester, & Short, 2009; Lanningham-Foster et al., 2006; Marks et al., 2005; Olmstead, 2007; Tan, Aziz, Chua, & Teh, 2002; Unnithan, Houser, & Fernhall, 2006; White, Lehmann, & Trent, 2007). It can also be a source of the more elusive moderate to vigorous intensity levels. Studies that gave teenagers more autonomy in their game decision making by allowing them to play as long as they wanted and at whatever level they wanted, showed higher levels of intensity (Weaver, Yang, & Foley, 2009; Yang & Foley, 2008; Yang & Graham, 2005). The research cited above (McGraw et al., 2005; Positive Gaming AB, 2010) suggests that beyond cardiovascular benefits, there may be visuo-spatial and short-term memory benefits as well.

DDR can be adapted for other modes of input as "steps," for example, the hand table shown in Fig. 4. Adaptations can be made by adapting an input device to any voluntary movement (hand, foot, knee, etc.). See Table 2 for other modifications to

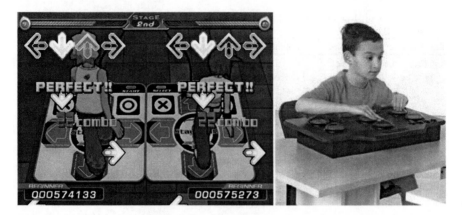

Fig. 3 Beginner level DDR feedback with DDR hand pad

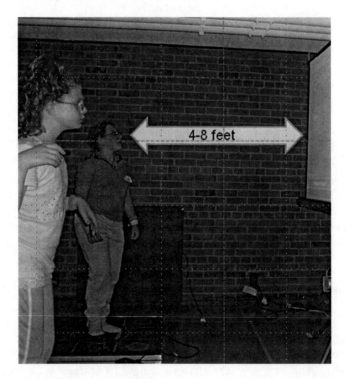

Fig. 4 Adapted *Dance Dance Revolution*

increase usability of *DDR* for youth with disabilities. For example, students with various visual impairments were able to successfully play *DDR* when an LCD projector was used to project the game onto a large screen and from a high angle (6 ft. off the ground, see Fig. 5) so that players could be placed close to the screen (Gasperetti

Table 2 Modifications to increase usability for DDR (adapted from Gasperetti et al., 2010)

Screen
- Use a large projector screen (standard classroom-sized, portable) or mount one to a wall
- Keep the animated dancer in the background for visual prompting and feedback
- Use a larger screen to create larger arrows
- Increase color contrast and enlarge letters
- Reduce room lighting for better contrast

Pads
- Shorten the distance between the dancer and the screen
- Turn the pads so that the user's better eye or usable eye can see the screen
- Set up practice pads and practice squares so the youth watching can practice
- Place tape on edge of arrow pad to mark arrows
- Allow students to wear socks or play barefoot to feel the pad

Projector
- Cover half of the projector lens if there is only one person working on the pads to eliminate some of the extra movement on the screen
- Place the projector on a 6-ft shelving unit or hang it from the ceiling in order to keep shadows off the screen

Practice
- Allow extra time, help, and more repetitions
- Have the youth start out by saying what direction the arrows are without moving their feet (e.g., "left, right, left, forward")
- Have the student voice "step" when they should be stepping without moving their feet

Gameplay
- Turn "booing" off
- Play until song ends, otherwise the game stops when your power level goes down
- Increase the size of arrows
- Add or remove virtual dancer
- Increase contrast of arrows for better visibility

et al., 2010). As one student remarked, "I really liked the size of the arrows that were going across the screen because they were big enough for me to see."

Sony PlayStation 2 EyeToy is another exergame that can be adapted for individuals with disabilities. It consists of a small web camera pointed at the player with all movements seen on screen as the character in the game (see Fig. 6). Players must move the entire body or specific body parts to play any of the games. The movements of the player, in response to the video game, result in a score for each game played. The more players succeed in completing their tasks (bouncing a ball, karate chopping, and cleaning windows) the more points they receive.

EyeToy is a fun family or group game because the players are on screen and not represented by a computerized action figure. In the truest sense, the player is part of the game.

Since its release in 2003, more game developers are incorporating EyeToy's unique USB camera sensor technology. Currently, there are 12 titles for games that use the EyeToy camera, including a personal trainer (*Kinetic*), karaoke singing and

Fig. 5 EyeToy Play 2 Table Tennis

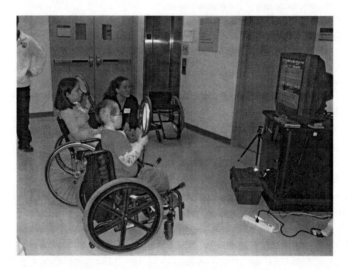

Fig. 6 Preparing to hit a virtual tennis ball in XaviX Tennis

dancing (*SingStar*), and hover board riding (*Antigrav*). *DDR Extreme* is a new game that combines all the foot pounding of traditional *DDR* with the arm movements of EyeToy. This ability to choose games, as well as the difficulty level, can increase one's sense of competence and autonomy.

EyeToy *Wishi Washi* is a game that many younger children like to play because it is simple. The objective is to clear off steamed up windows – represented by "steam" on the monitor or screen – by waving one's arms. Players try different strategies like running across the screen, jumping up and down, or getting closer to the camera which enables smaller movements to be effective. EyeToy *Boxing Chump* is a one-on-one three-round match up with a robot boxer. It is a full-body game which comes complete with blocking techniques, 8 s counts, and bonus points for landing combos. EyeToy *Kung Foo* is a fast-paced game with flying, attacking ninjas the players have to hit before they get too close. Some players slap them away, others karate chop, while others head butt or kick them. The longer a player stays alive, the faster and more frequent the ninjas come.

To date there have been seven studies that have investigated the impact of EyeToy Play or Play2 on physical activity levels and most of them found a moderate intensity effect (Aquino et al., 2006; Jannink et al., 2008; Lanningham-Foster et al., 2006; Lian, Astrid, & Toni, 2005; Maddison et al., 2007; Mhurchu et al., 2008; Yang & Foley, 2008). However, when children and teens are given the opportunity to choose their own games (exercise autonomy), the intensity can also be moderate to vigorous intensity (Weaver et al., 2009; Yang & Foley, 2008). According to five studies, using the more fitness-based EyeToy *Kinetic* activities seems to elicit moderate to vigorous intensities, in part because of the wide-angle camera that requires full-body movements in order to play (Alsac, Johnson, & Swan, 2007; Böhm, Hartmann, & Böhm, 2008; Gasperetti, Foley, Yang, Columna, Lieberman (2011); Thin, Howey, Murdoch, & Crozier, 2007; Weaver et al., 2009).

EyeToy's advantage is its unique user interface, projecting the player onto the screen, and the ability to use any body part or object to interact with the game elements. Currently, it is the only commercially available game that incorporates the actual game player into the video game. By the end of 2010, both Sony and Nintendo will have new peripherals that will use a camera, Move and Kinect, respectively. See Table 3 for modifications to increase usability of the EyeToy for youth with disabilities.

XaviX. A new exergame system that does not use a traditional video game console is XaviX (SSD Company Limited). Released in the USA in 2005, this represents an alternative game system that is marketed as a way to interact with onscreen video game action. XaviX games require a XaviXPORT game console, which plugs into the video input jacks on a television, and a XaviX game cartridge that comes with a specially modified sports accessory that serves as the game controller. For example, in XaviX® *Tennis*, participants will swing a small 12″ racquet to hit a moving tennis ball on the TV screen. The speed, angle and trajectory of the virtual ball will be determined by the player's swing. On the racquet are small infrared sensors that interact with the XaviXPORT motion sensing technology. These sensors detect players' actions and respond with appropriate onscreen action (see Fig. 6).

Very few studies have reviewed its effects on physical activity, but from the four identified research projects, it appears that XaviX games elicit moderate intensity physical activity (Bailey et al., 2008; Brandt, Haddock, Wilkin, & So, 2006; Mellecker & McManus, 2008; Weaver et al., 2009).

Using XaviX in APE follows many of the modifications listed above; however, when using the sporting equipment peripherals, there are some other considerations. Be sure that the batteries that are installed are new as it can be frustrating not to be able to play the game. Place the XaviX PORT at an unobstructed level that will be able to receive the infrared signals being reflected from the game peripherals.

Table 3 Modifications to increase usability for EyeToy Kinetic (adapted from Gasperetti et al., 2010)

Screen
- Use a large projector screen (standard classroom-sized, portable) or mount one to a wall
- Shorten the distance between the player and the screen
- Increase color contrast
- Reduce room lighting for better contrast

Camera
- Place camera as close to player as necessary and adjust the height
- Place tape on the floor to "mark" correct floor placement and camera position
- Allow students to wear socks or play barefoot to feel the tape on the floor

Projector
- Place the projector on a 6-ft shelving unit or hang it from the ceiling in order to keep shadows off the screen
- Use a bright light source placed on the floor pointing up at the player to increase visibility and contrast, allowing the camera to detect movements

Practice
- Allow extra time, help, and more repetitions
- Give auditory cues as indications of where the target is located. For example, if the target is to the right and high, a support person would clap right and high, etc.
- Give visual cues such as a red flag, a yellow ribbon, or a black scarf to indicate the target position
- Support the play of deaf and blind children by tapping the child's arm or leg depending on where the target is. Tap the child's back when the level is complete

Gameplay
- Use a good speaker system to reinforce in-game sounds and feedback, which reflect intensity of force. If the speakers are loud enough, they provide vibration feedback
- Use objects to give players another way to interact with the game
- Have an assistant hide from the camera but assist the player in moving his or her limbs and upper body to keep players with limited mobility involved with the games

The Nintendo Wii game console was released in November 2006 to great demand. The Wii was the first major gaming system to emphasize physical interactions with virtual worlds by the use of a wireless controller that has a traditional set of buttons, but its accelerometers and infrared sensors help to determine the controller's position in space. The multiple sensors allow players to move quite freely through the air.

To date there have been 16 studies that have analyzed the impact of playing *Wii Sports* on energy expenditure (Bailey et al., 2008; Bausch, Beran, Cahanes, & King, 2008; Böhm et al., 2008; Graves, Ridgers, & Stratton, 2008; Graves, Stratton, Ridgers, & Cable, 2007; Lyons et al., 2009; Miyachi, Yamamoto, Ohkawara, & Tanaka, 2009; Nitz, Kuys, Isles, & Fu, 2009; Pasch, Bianchi-Berthouze, van Dijk, & Nijholt, 2009; Penko & Barkley, 2010; Penko & Barkley, 2009; Porcari, Schmidt, & Foster, 2008; Saposnik et al., 2009; Westcombe, 2009; Willems & Bond, 2009a, 2009b). Most studies found that players of all ages played at the low to moderate levels of intensity; but a few studies had players performing some of the time in the moderate to vigorous intensities (Gasperetti et al., 2010). The two most popular games tend to be tennis and boxing (see Fig. 7).

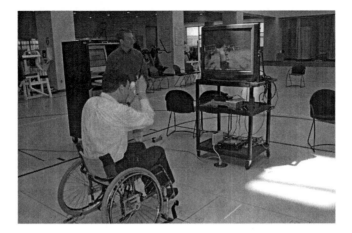

Fig. 7 Wii Boxing in a wheelchair on a force platform

To jump further into the world of physical gaming, Nintendo released *Wii Fit* in May 2008 which uses a wireless balance board to control gaming interactions and track BMI. This new gaming peripheral and software quickly became one of the Nintendo's most popular titles. Worldwide sales estimate about 22.5 million unit of *Wii Fit* have been sold (http://www.vgchartz.com). To date there have only been a handful of studies using the *Wii Fit* board and most of them have investigated its use as a form of balance training or therapy (Brumels, Blasius, Cortright, Oumedian, & Solberg, 2008; Clark et al., 2010; Hanneton & Varenne, 2009; Miyachi et al., 2009; Shih, Shih, & Chiang, 2010); only one study has examined its effect on energy expenditure on adults (Miyachi et al., 2009).

An exergame that is only available on the Wii is a fitness-based title called *EA SPORTS Active* and its sequel *EA SPORTS Active: More Workouts* which have collectively sold three million copies since their launch date in May 2009 (http://www.vgchartz.com). The game has the player to choose a male or female trainer to guide through a series of workouts using the two Wii controllers (Wiimote and nunchuck), resistance band, and/or the *Wii Fit* board. No studies have been reported on this title yet, but by looking at the sales and popularity of its social networking and support structure, it is only a matter of time before results start to appear.

Guitar Hero (Activision Publishing, Inc.) is a game played with a guitar-shaped controller on which players play chords and strum according to the music and rhythm of popular rock music. Ordinarily, all the directions appear in colored codes on the screen. Users with visual impairments typically have difficulty in playing. One researcher has developed several prototypes to address the needs of the visually impaired by using vibrotactile and auditory interface as opposed to the standard graphic user interface. One of the adaptations is a haptic glove (see Fig. 8) (Bei & Eelke, 2008).

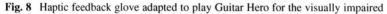

Fig. 8 Haptic feedback glove adapted to play Guitar Hero for the visually impaired

Games like *Guitar Hero* can be beneficial in improving fine motor skills, timing, and rhythm. The glove created by Bei and Eelke provides vibrations in the finger-tips that are to be pressed on the game controller (the guitar-shaped controller) to play along with the music, replicating in haptic feedback the chord fingering codes. This type of adaptations has also been tried with a tennis game using Wii remotes that provides vibrotactile and auditory feedback to cue the player when to swing and on which side (forehand or backhand). When playing this tennis game, children with severe visual impairments were able to achieve physical activity levels in the moderate zone and improve their motor coordination (Morelli, Foley, Columna, Lieberman, & Folmer, 2010).

The Future of Exergames

The income that exergames have generated is estimated to be approximately one billion dollars, most of which has been within the past couple of years (Bogost, Chamberlain, Flynn, Medina, & Yang, 2010). Only 3 years ago, Nintendo Wii was released and in that short period it has gone on to dominate game console sales by selling 70 million units, almost twice as many as Sony PS3 or Microsoft Xbox 360. Given the industry's motto, *Once a gamer, always a gamer*, the economic future of exergames seems assured.

Two major trends to watch in exergaming are controller/user interface innovations and multiplayer platforms. The next generation of game controllers will bring more immersive play with more sensitive and accurate motion tracking which will result in more feedback to the player. However, there remain concerns that accessibility is not being built into the new generation of controllers and most of these full-body active games will *assume* full mobility and range of motion. In June 2009, the Nintendo Wii *Motion Plus* was released, which allows for more accurate motion tracking while using the Nintendo Wii controller.

In June 2010 at the international game show, E3, other game console makers announced their newest advances for motion gaming. Microsoft's Xbox 360 *Kinect* (formerly known as *Project Natal*) was released in the fall of 2010. It has "skeletal mapping" that reads the motion of 48 points on the human body – assuming that the player is standing and has full range of motion. Sony's newest controller was announced, the Playstation *Move* for the PS3, to be released in the fall of 2010, with two new handheld controllers in conjunction with the Playstation Eye that will feature 1:1 motion tracking that will be calibrated to the player's movement ability.

Positive performance feedback (computer-generated) is another area of interface innovation. All new generation game controllers have vibration feedback built-in and some games are delivering feedback through peripherals. This type of feedback can be useful for gameplay and also better imitates the real-life experience. In some games, feedback is delivered through the game controller in the form of vibration (haptic) or sound. A peripheral compression vest can simulate shots to the body (see http://www.tngames.com). A fitness bike that looks like a standard stationary exercise bike, *MOG*, provides force-feedback (vibrations) in the handles, seat, and pedals. Another device featuring force-feedback is the *ForceTek XIO*, unveiled at the E3 conference in 2010 (http://www.forcetekusa.com/). It features a force-feedback game controller built into a wearable exoskeleton with tiny servos at each joint. The company plans on producing similar controllers for the shoulders and lower body to enhance the virtual interaction. This type of system has some interesting implications for rehabilitation, physical therapy, and kids with disabilities because it gives the player the sensation of an actual movement/performance, with the potential to reinforce the appropriate movement patterns for a given activity.

Many gaming experts feel that online gaming, a trend that opens up competitions and multiplayer training, is an area that will continue to drive the gaming industry (Deloitte Telecommunications Media and Technology (TMT) Group and Deloitte Research, 2004; Entertainment Software Association, 2004). Presently, there are numerous versions that allow more students to engage in DDR-type games simultaneously. The dance-game market has several multiplayer systems including Positive Gaming's *iDANCE*, which can accommodate 32 players on wireless pads and 32 players per screen, and Cobalt Flux's *BluFit*, which can accommodate 64 players on wireless pads, with 4 players per screen. There are obvious benefits to players of having their own dance pads and choosing their own level of difficulty, thus ensuring equal opportunities to students of all abilities. In addition, these game systems allow teachers to track student performance on a short- or long-term basis by having all scores downloadable to a spreadsheet. One system in development will feature an online network that will enable administrators, teachers, students, parents, and researchers access to the data. The software will capture players' step counts, accuracy, points, and even their mood (happy faces) at the end of their session.

EA Sports has leveraged the Internet with a strong social networking component for *EA Sports Active*. Players can network with friends, receive technical and personal trainer support, and get up-to-date information on new title releases. Another company that has embraced an online community is Ubisoft's *Your Shape: Fitness Evolved*. The product has not yet been released and their Facebook group already has more than 36,000 "fans." As Bonsignore et al. (this volume) describe that such social networks can provide opportunities for individuals to find communities of interest and support that enhance their personal and professional goals.

Youth with disabilities need to be more active. Reaching this goal will require more members of the community to be involved. One of the most important advocates for physical activity can be local health care providers. The Academy of Pediatrics advises physicians to promote participation in physical activity for all children (Murphy & Carbone, 2008). Their position is that physical activity, sport, and recreation benefits all children, and that children with disabilities are no exception. This aligns with personalized education and the use of inclusive technology in helping students learn in multiple environments. Adapted PE is an obvious environment to build skills and habits for a more active lifestyle and exergames are an engaging and promising new instructional alternative. The chart of advocacy resources included in Appendix A can be utilized by educators, parents, and health care providers to build momentum for getting kids moving with exergames.

Appendix A: Advocacy and Resources for Game Accessibility (Adapted from IGDA, 2004)

Name	Description	URL
AbleGamers Foundation	Advocacy for the disabled in the realm of digital entertainment	http://www.ablegamersfoundation.org
All in play	Accessible online games	http://www.allinplay.com/home.html
AudioGames	News and reviews of audio games	http://www.audiogames.net/
Audussey Magazine	Games accessible to the blind	http://www.audysseymagazine.org/
BBC Ouch!	BBC's site about accessible games	http://www.bbc.co.uk/ouch/closeup/ gaming.shtml
BSC Games	Games for blind and visually impaired	http://www.bscgames.com/
Blind Gamers at Yahoo	Very active e-mail list	http://gamesource.groups.yahoo.com/ group/blindgamers/
Closed Captioning	Article about closed captioning in games	http://www.rbkdesign.com/game/ articles/captioning.php
Deaf Gamers	Game reviews from the deaf perspective	www.deafgamers.com
ESP Softworks	Games accessible for the visually impaired	http://www.espsoftworks.com/
Games For the Blind	Games for the blind	http://www.gamesfortheblind.com/
Games for Health	Games for Health initiative	http://www.gamesforhealth.org
GMA Games	Games for blind and visually impaired	http://www.gmagames.com/

(continued)

(continued)

Name	Description	URL
Gone Gold	FAQ about gamers with disabilities	http://www.gonegold.com/misc/gwd/
IGDA Game Accessibility SIG	The game accessibility special interest group at International Game Developers Association	http://www.igda.org/accessibility/
Level Games	Games accessible for motor impairments	http://www.levelgames.net/
Pin Interactive	Developer of *Terraformers* – accessible 3D graphic game	http://www.pininteractive.com/
Shoot	Speech recognition program	http://clans.gameclubcentral.com/shoot/
SonoKids	Accessible music games	http://www.sonokids.com/wwwsonokids/english/index.html
Sound Support	Audio games	http://www.soundsupport.net/
Textmode Quake	The game *Quake* in text mode	http://webpages.mr.net/bobz/ttyquake/

References

Abbott, M., McElroy, C., & Ruocco, J. (2009). *A comparison of heart rate, caloric expenditure and rating of perceived exertion while playing the Wii Fit free run against jogging on a treadmill.* Cortland: State University of New York College at Cortland.

Alsac, B., Johnson, L., & Swan, P. (2007). Cardiovascular response to an activity-based video game in a college-age population. *Medicine & Science in Sports & Exercise, 39*(5 Suppl), S198.

American Association for Active Lifestyles and Fitness. (2004). *A position statement on including students with disabilities in physical education.* VA: Reston.

Aquino, A., Balestri, E., Dall'Ara, S., Lami, I., Gobbi, E., Ambroni, M., et al. (2006). Efficacy of physical exercise playing a video game for mucus clearance in patients with Cystic Fibrosis. *Journal of Cystic Fibrosis, 5*(Suppl 1), S83–S189.

Arciero, P., Anderson-Hanley, C., Nimon, J., Westen, S., DeMatteo, L., Okuma, N., & Klein, R. (2009, April). *Physiological Effects of Videogame-enhanced Exercise for Older Adults: Results from the Cybercycle Study.* Paper presented at the annual meeting of the Society of Behavioral Medicine, Montreal, Canada.

Bailey, B., Marcelus, F., Lujares, M., Kennard, L., & McInnis, K. (2008). Energy cost of exergaming in adolescents. *Obesity, 16*(1), S77.

Bausch, L., Beran, J., Cahanes, S., & King, L. (2008). Physiological responses while playing Nintendo Wii Sports. *Journal of Undergraduate Kinesiology Research, 3*(2), 19–25.

Bei, Y., & Eelke, F. (2008). *Blind hero: enabling guitar hero for the visually impaired.* Paper presented at the Proceedings of the 10th international ACM SIGACCESS conference on Computers and accessibility.

Bethell, C., Read, D., Blumberg, S., & Newacheck, P. (2008). What is the prevalence of children with special health care needs? Toward an understanding of variations in findings and methods across three national surveys. *Maternal and Child Health Journal, 12*, 1–14.

Bierre, K. (2005). Improving game accessibility. Retrieved from http://www.gamasutra.com/features/20050706/bierre_01.shtml.

Boffoli, N., & Foley, J. T. (2010). Enjoyment levels of youth with visual impairments while playing exergames. *Research Quarterly for Exercise and Sport, 81*(1), A-88–A-89.

Bogost, I., Chamberlain, B., Flynn, S., Medina, E., & Yang, S. P. (2010). *Over a billion dollars can't be wrong: is exergaming success a victory for serious games?* Paper presented at the Game Developers Conference, San Francisco, CA.

Böhm, H., Hartmann, M., & Böhm, B. (2008). *Predictors of metabolic energy expenditure from body acceleration and mechanical energies in new generation active computer games.* Paper presented at the IACSS – Computer Science in Sport, Schloss Dagstuhl – Leib.

Brandt, A. M., Haddock, B. L., Wilkin, L. D., & So, H. (2006). *The use of interactive video games for exercise in children.* Paper presented at the SWACSM, San Diego, CA.

Brumels, K. A., Blasius, T., Cortright, T., Oumedian, D., Solberg, B. (2008). Comparison of efficacy between traditional and video game based balance programs. *Clin Kinesiol, 62*(4):26–31.

Burgeson, C. R., Wechsler, H., Brener, N. D., Young, J. C., & Spain, C. G. (2001). Physical education and activity: results from the School Health Policies and Programs Study 2000. *Journal of School Health, 71*(7), 279–293.

Centers for Disease Control and Prevention. (2010). *The association between school-based physical activity, including physical education, and academic performance.* Atlanta, GA: U.S. Department of Health and Human Services.

Clark, R. A., Bryant, A. L., Pua, Y., McCrory, P., Bennell, K., & Hunt, M. (2010). Validity and reliability of the Nintendo Wii Balance Board for assessment of standing balance. *Gait & Posture, 31*(3), 307–310.

Datar, A., Sturm, R., & Magnabosco, J. L. (2004). Childhood overweight and academic performance: national study of kindergartners and first-graders. *Obesity Research, 12*(1), 58–68.

Deloitte Telecommunications Media and Technology (TMT) Group and Deloitte Research. (2004). *Moore's Law and electronic games. How technology advance will take electronic games everywhere.* New York: Deloitte Research.

Deutsch, J. E., Borbely, M., Filler, J., Huhn, K., & Guarrera-Bowlby, P. (2008). Use of a low-cost, commercially available gaming console (Wii) for rehabilitation of an adolescent with cerebral palsy. *Physical Therapy, 88*(10), 1196–1207.

Drowatzky, J. N., Geiger, W. L. (1993). Cluster analysis of intelligence, age, and motor ability performance of mentally retarded and non-mentally retarded children. *Clinical Kinesiology, 46*(4), 7–11.

Entertainment Software Association. (2004). Essential facts about the computer and video game industry. *2004 Sales, demographics and usage data.* Retrieved December 1, 2004, from http://www.theesa.com/EFBrochure.pdf.

Entertainment Software Association. (2009). Essential facts about the computer and video game industry. *2009 Sales, demographics and usage data.* Retrieved December 1, 2009, from http://www.theesa.com/EFBrochure.pdf.

Fernhall, B., & Unnithan, V. B. (2002). Physical activity, metabolic issues, and assessment. *Physical Medicine and Rehabilitation Clinics of North America, 13*(4), 925–947.

Flynn, S., Palma, P., & Bender, A. (2007). Feasibility of using the Sony PlayStation 2 gaming platform for an individual poststroke: a case report. *Journal of Neurologic Physical Therapy, 31*(4), 180–189.

Foley, J. T., Harvey, S., Chun, H. J., & Kim, S. Y. (2008). The relationships among fundamental motor skills, health-related physical fitness, and body fatness in South Korean adolescents with mental retardation. *Research Quarterly for Exercise and Sport, 79*(2), 149–157.

Gasperetti, B., Foley, J. T., Yang, S. P., Columna, L., Lieberman, L. (2011). Comparison of three exergames played by youth with visual impairments. *Research Quarterly for Exercise and Sport, 82*(1), A.

Gasperetti, B., Milford, M., Blanchard, D., Yang, S., Lieberman, L., & Foley, J. (2010). Dance dance revolution and eye toy kinetic modifications for youths with visual impairments. *The Journal of Physical Education, Recreation & Dance, 81*(4), 15–17. 55.

Golomb, M.R., McDonald, B.C., Warden, S.J., Yonkman, J., Saykim, A.J., Shirley, B., Huber, M., Rabin, B., AdelBaky, M., Nwosu, M., Barkat-Masih, M., Burdea, G. (2010). In-home virtual reality videogame telerehabilitation in adolescents with hemiplegic cerebral palsy. *Archives of Physical Medicine and Rehabilitation, 91*(1), 1–8.e1.

Graf, C., Koch, B., Dordel, S., Schindler-Marlow, S., Icks, A., Schuller, A., et al. (2004). Physical activity, leisure habits and obesity in first-grade children. *European Journal of Cardiovascular Prevention and Rehabilitation, 11*(4), 284–290.

Graf, D. L., Pratt, L. V., Hester, C. N., & Short, K. R. (2009). Playing active video games increases energy expenditure in children. *Pediatrics, 124*(2), 534–540.

Graves, L., Ridgers, N., & Stratton, G. (2008). The contribution of upper limb and total body movement to adolescents' energy expenditure whilst playing Nintendo Wii. *European Journal of Applied Physiology, 104*(4), 617–623.

Graves, L., Stratton, G., Ridgers, N. D., & Cable, N. T. (2007). Comparison of energy expenditure in adolescents when playing new generation and sedentary computer games: cross sectional study. *BMJ, 335*(7633), 1282–1284.

Hanneton, S., & Varenne, A. (2009). *Coaching the Wii: Evaluation of a physical training experiment assisted by a video game.* Paper presented at the Haptic, Audio, Visual Environments and Games (HAVE 2009), Lecco, Italy.

Healthy People 2010. (2004). *Progress Review: Physical Activity and Fitness.* Retrieved from http://www.healthypeople.gov/data/2010prog/focus22/2004fa22.htm.

International Game Developers Association (2004). *Accessibility in games: Motivations and approaches.* Retrieved from http://archives.igda.org/accessibility/IGDA_Accessibility_WhitePaper.pdf.

Jannink, M. J. A., van der Wilden, G. J., Navis, D. W., Visser, G., Gussinklo, J., & Ijzerman, M. (2008). A low-cost video game applied for training of upper extremity function in children with cerebral palsy: a pilot study. *CyberPsychology & Behavior, 11*(1), 27–32.

Kalapanidas, E., Davarakis, C., Fernández-Aranda, F., Jiménez-Murcia, S., Kocsis, O., Ganchev, T., et al. (2009). PlayMancer: games for health with accessibility in mind. *Communications & Strategies, 1*(73), 105–120.

Kim, H. K., Matsuura, Y., Tanaka, K., & Inagaki, A. (1993). Physical fitness and motor ability in obese boys 12 through 14 years of age. *Annals of Physiological Anthropology, 12*(1), 17–23.

Lanningham-Foster, L., Jensen, T. B., Foster, R. C., Redmond, A. B., Walker, B. A., Heinz, D., et al. (2006). Energy expenditure of sedentary screen time compared with active screen time for children. *Pediatrics, 118*(6), e1831–e1835.

Lesher, K., & Monasterio, E. (2004). Video game playing habits of children with disabilities. *Archives of Physical Medicine and Rehabilitation, 85*(9), e44.

Lian, L., Astrid, T. L., & Toni, R. (2005). *Labanotation for design of movement-based interaction.* Paper presented at the Proceedings of the second Australasian conference on Interactive entertainment, Sydney, Australia.

Lyons, E., Tate, D., Erickson, K., Vaughn, A., Grabow, M., & Ward, D. (2009). Energy expenditure during Wii Sports minigames in overweight children: comparing data parameter selection. *Obesity, 16*(1), S78.

Maddison, R., Mhurchu, C. N., Jull, A., Jiang, Y., Prapavessis, H., & Rodgers, A. (2007). Energy expended playing video console games: an opportunity to increase children's physical activity? *Pediatric Exercise Science, 19*(3), 334–343.

Marks, J., Maloney, A., Bethea, T., Kelsey, K., Rosenberg, A., Paez, S., et al. (2005, June 16–18). *Can an active video game decrease sedentary screen time among children?* Paper presented at the Fourth Annual Conference of the International Society of Behavioral Nutrition and Physical Activity (ISBNPA), Amsterdam, The Netherlands.

Matysczok, C., Radkowski, R., & Berssenbruegge, J. (2004). AR-bowling: immersive and realistic game play in real environments using augmented reality. *2004 ACM SIGCHI International Conference on Advances in Computer Entertainment Technology* (pp. 269–276). Singapore: ACM Press.

McGraw, T., Burdette, K., & Chadwick, K. (2005). *The effects of a consumer-oriented multimedia game on the reading disorders of children with ADHD.* Paper presented at the DiGRA 2005: Changing Views: Worlds in Play, Vancouver, British Columbia, Canada.

Mellecker, R. R., & McManus, A. M. (2008). Energy expenditure and cardiovascular responses to seated and active gaming in children. *Archives of Pediatrics & Adolescent Medicine, 162*(9), 886–891.

Mhurchu, C. N., Maddison, R., Jiang, Y., Jull, A., Prapavessis, H., & Rodgers, A. (2008). Couch potatoes to jumping beans: a pilot study of the effect of active video games on physical activity in children. *International Journal of Behavioral Nutrition and Physical Activity, 5*, 8.

Miyachi, M., Yamamoto, K., Ohkawara, K., & Tanaka, S. (2009). Energy expenditure in adults when playing next-generation video games: a metabolic chamber study. *Circulation, 120*(18), S433.

Morelli, T., Foley, J., Columna, L., Lieberman, L., & Folmer, E. (2010). *VI-Tennis: a vibrotactile/audio exergame for players who are visually impaired*. Paper presented at the Foundations of Digital Interactive Games (FDG), Monterey, California.

Mulye, T. P., Park, M. J., Nelson, C. D., et al. (2009). Trends in adolescent and young adult health in the United States. *Journal of Adolescent Health 45*(1), 8–24.

Murphy, N. A., & Carbone, P. S. (2008). Promoting the participation of children with disabilities in sports, recreation, and physical activities. *Pediatrics, 121*(5), 1057–1061.

Nitz, J. C., Kuys, S., Isles, R., & Fu, S. (2009). Is the Wii Fit a new-generation tool for improving balance, health and well-being? A pilot study. *Climacteric, 13*(5), 487–491.

Obama, M. (2010). *First Lady Michelle Obama Launches Let's Move: America's Move to Raise a Healthier Generation of Kids*. Retrieved from http://www.whitehouse.gov/the-press-office/first-lady-michelle-obama-launches-lets-move-americas-move-raise-a-healthier-genera.

Ogden, C. L., Carroll, M. D., Curtin, L. R., Lamb, M. M., & Flegal, K. M. (2010). Prevalence of high body mass index in US children and adolescents, 2007-2008. *JAMA, 303*(3), 242–249.

Ohshima, T., Satoh, K., Yamamoto, H., & Tamura, H. (1998). *AR2 Hockey: a case study of collaborative augmented reality*. Paper presented at the 1998 IEEE Virtual Reality Annual International Symposium.

Okely, A. D., Booth, M., & Patterson, J. (2001). Relationship of physical activity to fundamental movement skills among adolescents. *Medicine and Science in Sports and Exercise, 33*(11), 1899–1904.

Olkin, R. (1999). *What psychotherapists should know about disability*. New York: Guilford Press.

Olmstead, B. (2007, June 24–27). *The effects of interactive video (DDR) on heart rate, perceived exertion, step count, and enjoyment in elementary school children*. Paper presented at the International Conference on physical activity and obesity in children, Toronto, Ontario, Canada.

Pasch, M., Bianchi-Berthouze, N., van Dijk, B., & Nijholt, A. (2009). Movement-based sports video games: Investigating motivation and gaming experience. *Entertainment Computing, 1*(2), 49–61.

Chin A Paw, M. J. M., Jacobs, W. M., Vaessena, E. P. G., Titzeb, S., & Mechelen, Wv. (2008). The motivation of children to play an active video game. *Journal of Science and Medicine in Sport, 11*(2), 163–166.

Penko, A., & Barkley, J. E. (2009). The physiologic effects and reinforcing value of playing a physically-interactive video game in children. *Medicine & Science in Sports & Exercise, 41*(5), 93.

Penko, A., & Barkley, J. (2010). Motivation and physiologic responses of playing a physically interactive video game relative to a sedentary alternative in children. *Annals of Behavioral Medicine, 39*(2), 162–169.

Physical Activity Guidelines Advisory Committee. (2008). *Physical Activity Guidelines Advisory Committee Report*. Washington, DC: U.S. Department of Health and Human Services.

Porcari, J., Schmidt, K., & Foster, C. (2008). As good as the real thing? ACE Fitness Matters, July/August, 7–9

Positive Gaming AB. (2010). *Positive Gaming iDANCE*. Eslöv, Sweden: Positive Gaming AB.

Prensky, M. (2001). The motivation of gameplay or, the REAL 21st century learning revolution. *The Horizon, 10*(1), 1–14.

Rideout, V. J., Foehr, U. G., & Roberts, D. F. (2010). *Generation M2: media in the lives of 8- to 18-year-olds*. Menlo Park, CA: Kaiser Family Foundation.

Roberts, D. F., Foehr, U. G., & Rideout, V. J. (2005). *Generation M: media in the lives of 8–18 year-olds*. Menlo Park: Henry J. Kaiser Family Foundation.

Robusto, K., & Nichols, J. (2010). *Metabolic responses to exergaming among older adults*. Paper presented at the San Diego State University 2010 Student Research Symposium, San Diego, CA.

Rosa, J., Rodriguez, L. P., & Marquez, S. (1996). Relacion entre actividad fisica y ejecucion motora en poblacion escolar. *Rehabilitacion, 30*, 187–193.

Saposnik, G., Bayley, M., Cheung, D., Willems, J., Mamdani, M., Cohen, L., et al. (2009). FP12-MO-04 Virtual reality technology in stroke rehabilitation: a pilot randomized trial using Wii gaming system. *Journal of the Neurological Sciences, 285*(Suppl. 1), S76.

Shih, C.-H., Shih, C.-T., & Chiang, M.-S. (2010). A new standing posture detector to enable people with multiple disabilities to control environmental stimulation by changing their standing posture through a commercial Wii Balance Board. *Research in Developmental Disabilities, 31*(1), 281–286.

Tan, B., Aziz, A. R., Chua, K., & Teh, K. C. (2002). Aerobic demands of the dance simulation game. *International Journal of Sports Medicine, 23*(2), 125–129.

Thin, A. G., Howey, D., Murdoch, L., & Crozier, A. (2007). *Evaluation of physical exertion required to play the body movement controlled Eyetoy Kinetic video game.* Paper presented at the Life Sciences, Glasgow, UK.

Tilinger, P., & Lejcarova, A. (2003). *Motor performance of mentally retarded boys and girls aged 14–15 years.* Paper presented at the European Conference of Mental Handicap and Elite Sports: Limits and Pertinence, Paris, France.

U.S. Department of Education. (2003). *Computer and internet use by children and adolescents in 2001.* Washington, DC: National Center for Education Statistics.

U.S. Department of Health and Human Services. (2005). *The Surgeon General's Call To Action To Improve the Health and Wellness of Persons with Disabilities.*

U.S. Department of Health & Human Services. (2008). *2008 Physical Activity Guidelines for Americans.* Washington, DC: U.S. Department of Health and Human Services.

U.S. Department of Health & Human Services. (2008). *The National Survey of Children with Special Health Care Needs Chartbook 2005–2006.* Rockville, MD. Retrieved February 8, 2011 from: http://cshcndata.org/DataQuery/DataQueryResults.aspx

Unnithan, V. B., Houser, W., & Fernhall, B. (2006). Evaluation of the energy cost of playing a dance simulation video game in overweight and non-overweight children and adolescents. *International Journal of Sports Medicine, 27*(10), 804–809.

Warburton, D. E., Bredin, S. S., Horita, L. T., Zbogar, D., Scott, J. M., Esch, B. T., et al. (2007). The health benefits of interactive video game exercise. *Applied Physiology, Nutrition, and Metabolism, 32*(4), 655–663.

Warburton, D. E. R., Sarkany, D., Johnson, M., Rhodes, R. E., Whitford, W., Esch, B. T. A., et al. (2009). Metabolic requirements of interactive video game cycling. *Medicine & Science in Sports & Exercise, 41*(4), 920–926.

Weaver, J. J., Yang, S. P., & Foley, J. T. (2009). *Comparison of MVPA while playing DDR, EyeToy Kinetic and XaviX Tennis.* Paper presented at the American Alliance for Health, Physical Education, Recreation and Dance, Tampa, Florida.

Westcombe, F. W. (2009). *How effective is the Nintendo Wii Fit game in delivering health benefits on aerobic fitness, body-fat composition and cholesterol compared to a traditional training regime.* Paper presented at the BASES 2009 Annual Student Conference, Kingston Upon Hull.

White, M., Lehmann, H., & Trent, M. (2007). Disco dance video game-based interventional study on childhood obesity. *Journal of Adolescent Health, 40*(2 Suppl. 1), S32.

Widman, L. M., McDonald, C. M., & Abresch, R. T. (2006). Effectiveness of an upper extremity exercise device integrated with computer gaming for aerobic training in adolescents with spinal cord dysfunction. *Journal of Spinal Cord Medicine, 29*(4), 363–370.

Willems, M., & Bond, T. (2009a). Comparison of physiological and metabolic responses to playing Nintendo Wii Sports and brisk treadmill walking. *Journal of Human Kinetics, 22*, 43–49.

Willems, M., & Bond, T. (2009b). Metabolic equivalent of brisk walking and playing new generation active computer games in young-adults. *Medicina Sportiva, 13*(2), 95–98.

Yang, S. P., & Foley, J. T. (2008). Comparison of MVPA while playing DDR and EyeToy. *Research Quarterly for Exercise and Sport, 79*(Suppl. 1), A-17.

Yang, S. P., & Graham, G. M. (2005). Project GAME (Gaming Activities for More Exercise). *Research Quarterly for Exercise and Sport, 76*(Suppl. 1), A-96.

Yang, S. P., Smith, B. K., & Graham, G. M. (2008). Healthy video gaming: oxymoron or possibility? Innovate, 4(4). Retrieved from http://innovateonline.info/pdf/vol4_issue4/Healthy_Video_Gaming-__Oxymoron_or_Possibility_.pdf

Personalizing Assessment

Michael Russell

Introduction

Personalization has become a powerful approach for engaging people with products and services. Today, our children can walk into a Build-A-Bear store and in minutes create a personalized stuffed animal. We can log onto Nike.com and build a pair of shoes using our favorite color patterns and slogans. With the click of a few buttons, we can access long lists of movies and television programs and select those that appeal to us to view on demand anytime, anywhere. Within minutes of creating a Pandora account, we can listen to a "radio station" tailored to our musical tastes. Each morning, we can wake to newswires that deliver stories specific to our interests. And, when searching for new books to read, Amazon can generate a list of recommendations based on our recent browsing behavior.

In the field of education, personalization is also gaining attention. As one example, the National Educational Technology Plan advocates for exploring and developing ways to personalize educational experiences for each individual student. In the field of special education, the idea of tailoring instruction and learning experiences to meet each individual's need is also firmly established. While a robust body of methods and tools for personalizing learning is not yet widely available, teaching and learning are moving rapidly in this direction.

When it comes to testing and assessment in elementary and secondary education, however, the concept and implementation of personalization has gained little traction. This is due, in part, to the inflexible nature of paper-based tests and to a tradition of administering tests under standardized conditions. This chapter provides an overview of the potential for assessment practice made possible by technology and a personalization approach. It will guide educators who advocate for accommodations or educate their colleagues on the topic; who serve on test adoption committees; and all who are interested in fairness in testing for students with disabilities.

M. Russell (✉)
Boston College, Boston, MA, USA
e-mail: russelmh@bc.edu

T. Gray and H. Silver-Pacuilla (eds.), *Breakthrough Teaching and Learning: How Educational and Assistive Technologies are Driving Innovation*, DOI 10.1007/978-1-4419-7768-7_7, © Springer Science+Business Media, LLC 2011

Traditional Testing

Traditional notions of testing hold that a test should be administered under standardized conditions. For many tests, standardized conditions mean that examinees respond to the same set of items (i.e., questions) presented in an identical manner, under the same time conditions, using the same tools to produce responses, and, ideally, in environments that are as similar as possible.

The focus on standardizing the conditions under which a test is performed is driven by important and legitimate concerns about test validity. At its core, test validity focuses on the accuracy of an inference about an examinee based on a test score and the appropriateness of subsequent decisions made based on that inference. To assure fairness, it is commonly believed that standardizing test conditions provides all examinees with the same opportunity to demonstrate their skills, knowledge, and understanding.

For many students, however, this belief does not hold. As one example, several studies provide evidence that students' choice of a writing tool has a significant effect on their performance on writing tests. Specifically, students who are accustomed to producing text using a word processor perform 0.5–1.0 standard deviations higher when they are able to use a computer during a writing test as compared to when they must produce a response on paper. Conversely, students who are accustomed to writing on paper perform significantly worse when they must take a writing test on a computer (Horkay, Bennett, Allen, Kaplan, & Yan, 2006; Russell, 1999; Russell & Haney, 1997; Russell & Plati, 2001). For writing tests, there is clear evidence that standardizing the condition in which students produce responses does not result in valid inferences about students' writing ability. Instead, standardizing conditions systematically harms validity for one group of students depending on the mode selected by the testing program.

A New Look at Assessment and Testing

Rather than standardizing test conditions, this chapter argues that personalizing assessments will enhance validity and provide more meaningful information about student learning. In the sections that follow, we explore the goals of improving the quality of information provided during assessment by personalizing the assessment experience. This exploration begins by distinguishing assessment from testing, and reinforcing the importance of testing the intended construct without interference. Next, we examine the concept of accessibility and, in the process, argue that universally designed computer-based tests hold potential to replace the notion of test accommodations with accessibility. The concept of accessibility is then expanded through an example of tailoring the content of test items and assessment tasks to increase engagement and provide more meaningful information about student learning. The chapter ends by revisiting the concept of validity and arguing that the benefits of personalized assessments outweigh the benefits of standardization.

How Does Testing Differ from Assessment?

References to testing and assessment have become nearly ubiquitous in the field of education. Too often, the terms are used interchangeably. This is unfortunate, because there are important differences between a test and an assessment. An *assessment* is a three-step process that involves collecting information, analyzing that information, and then making a decision; a *test* is an instrument developed to measure a specific set of cognitive skills or knowledge. Table 1 provides a brief glossary of the terms used in this chapter to clarify the key underlying concepts of testing and assessment. Interested readers can find more explanations of these concepts in Airasian and Russell (2008).

Table 1 Glossary of terms

Accommodation	Support provided to students which are designed to reduce the impact of the unintended construct without changing the intended construct measured by the item
Adaptation	A change to a test item that alters the construct measured by the item
Assessment	A three-step process that involves collecting information, making use of that information, and then making a decision
Construct	A set of cognitive processes that occur within the brain, e.g., ability to perform addition
Intended construct	The skills and knowledge one is trying to measure
Unintended construct	Skills and abilities that one is *not* trying to measure but that may interfere with the measure of the intended construct, such as word decoding skills with math word problems
Item or task	Information that establishes a problem or a context designed to stimulate or activate the intended construct
Response	A product produced by a student that provides observable evidence of the outcome of the application of the intended construct, e.g., selection of an option, filling in a blank or essay, or an oral answer
Standardized test conditions	The protocol which guides test delivery, usually requiring examinees to respond to the same set of items (i.e., questions), presented in an identical manner, under the same time conditions, using the same tools to produce responses, and, ideally, in environments that are as similar as possible
Test	An instrument developed to measure a specific set of cognitive skills or knowledge
Validity	The extent to which the test provides an accurate measure of a given construct and allows for accurate inferences about a construct

As we explore the concept of personalization, we give careful consideration to *personalizing test items and administration conditions*. This approach has several advantages, such as:

- Maximizing accurate understanding of the test item by the student
- Activating the students' understanding of the construct
- Minimizing interference from other competing constructs
- Allowing responses that accurately reflect students' understanding

Understanding the concept of a *construct* more fully will illustrate how test accommodations and accessibility can help improve the measure of a construct. At its core, educational testing is about measuring constructs – the skills, knowledge, and understanding that are the intention of instruction. That is, did the student learn what was taught? Making inferences about the extent to which a construct operates within a student requires careful thought to define it, determine what constitutes evidence of the construct, and skills or abilities that may interfere with the measure of the intended construct.

In classroom contexts, teachers may provide a variety of supports designed to meet students' needs as they develop understanding of an intended construct. In many cases, these supports take the form of instructional strategies, learning activities, or other changes that the teacher may make to the classroom environment, the material, or the way he or she presents information to make it more accessible for students. Oftentimes, these supports are designed to decrease the influence that one or more unintended constructs have on the development of the intended construct. As an example, reading aloud text contained in a mathematics word problem reduces the effect that reading ability (an unintended construct) has on the development of mathematical ability (the intended construct). Similarly, a large-scale testing program may provide supports designed to minimize the influence that unintended constructs have on the intended construct. In both classroom and large-scale testing contexts, the supports provided to students which are designed to reduce the impact of the unintended construct – yet do not change the intended construct one is trying to measure – are referred to as *accommodations*.

Accommodations are designed to support a student in three stages of interaction with a test: access to test content, interactions with content, and response to content. Accessing content requires information presented in a given form to be internalized by the student. Interactions with content require students to process, assimilate, manipulate, and/or interpret content that has been internalized. Responding requires students to produce an observable product that is the outcome of their interaction with content. During each of these three stages, unintended constructs can interfere with a student's ability to access, interact, and respond in a manner that allows him/her to either develop the intended construct or for an assessment task to measure the intended construct.

Over the past 30 years, most discussions about accommodations have focused on a specific method used to meet a need. While methods are important, the essential aspect of an accommodation is the specific need that must be met in order to decrease the influence of an unintended construct.

Categories of Accommodations

Traditionally, accommodations have been classified into five categories, each of which captures the *type of change* made to test content, or the conditions under which a test is administered. These five categories include changes in: (a) presentation; (b) equipment and/or materials; (c) response methods; (d) schedule and timing; and (e) setting (Thurlow et al., 2000). When viewed from the perspectives of accessibility needs, accommodations can be re-classified into four categories of *student need*: (1) presentation needs; (2) interaction needs; (3) response needs; and (4) representational form needs. This section provides examples that address each type of accessibility need.

Adapted Presentation

In a test, content is most often transmitted in print form from paper or a computer to the student, but sometimes oral transmission is employed. When presented in print on paper or computer, a student's visual perception ability can interfere with the transmission of content. As an example, a student with low vision or dyslexia may experience difficulty in perceiving content presented in 12-point font or when presented as black text on a white background.

To minimize the influence that these unintended constructs have on the transmission of content, the presentation of that content may be adapted to meet the student's presentation need. Adapted presentation focuses on changes to the way in which test content is presented to a student. Examples of adapted presentation include changing the font size used to present text-based content, altering the contrast of text and images, increasing white space, and reducing the amount of content presented on a page. As discussed in greater detail later, a variety of methods and tools for adapting the presentation of content can be built into a technology-based test delivery system.

Adapted Interactions

Interaction needs focus on the processing of information to develop new knowledge, deepen understanding, respond to questions, or solve problems. When responding to stimuli presented by a test item, a variety of unintended constructs can interfere with the processing of information. As a few examples, a student's ability to remain focused, monitor his or her pace, recognize and focus on relevant information, organize information, maintain sufficient motivation and energy levels, and remain comfortable in the setting can all interfere with a student's interaction with content.

To minimize the influence that these unintended constructs have on interactions with test content, the conditions under which a student interacts with content may be adapted to meet the student's interaction needs. Examples of adapted interactions include assisting students with pacing, masking content, and scaffolding. For paper-based materials, adapted interactions often require students to work directly with an adult and/or with additional materials, such as templates or masks (covers that expose only a portion of the content at a time and thereby reduce distractions). For a technology-based test delivery system, adapted interaction tools can be built into the delivery interface.

Adapted Response Modes

Response needs focus on generating a product in response to a given task, question, or test item. A variety of needs that are unrelated to the targeted construct may affect a student's ability to produce a response that represents his or her current knowledge, understanding, or skill level. As a few examples, gross and fine motor skills, word production skills, and language skills can all interfere with the production of responses.

Adapted response modes focus on the method a student uses to provide responses to assess tasks. Examples of adapted response modes include: producing text either orally to a scribe or by using speech-to-text software; pointing to answers or using a touch screen instead of circling, clicking, or bubbling; or using assistive communication devices to produce responses. For paper-based assessment tasks, adapted response modes may require a student to interact with a scribe to produce a permanent record of their response. For tasks and items presented in a digital format, a delivery system could allow students to use a variety of assistive technologies connected to the computer (e.g., touch screen, single switch devices, alternate keyboards, speech-to-text software, eye-tracking software, etc.) that enable students to produce responses.

Tailored Representational Forms

A student's ability to perceive and process content can be influenced by the form in which the content is presented. As an example, a student who is blind cannot access content presented in print-based form. However, when that same content is presented in Braille, the content becomes accessible for the student (assuming the student is a Braille reader). Similarly, content presented in oral form may be difficult to access for a student with a hearing need. However, when presented through sign language, the content becomes accessible.

This final aspect of accessibility needs focuses on tailoring the representational form used to present content so that the student is better able to recognize and process that content. Mislevy et al. (2010) explained that several different representational forms can be used to present instructional or test content to a student.

To enable a student to recognize and process content, the form used to present that content may need to be tailored based on the student's representational form need. Unlike adapted presentations, which manipulate the way in which identical content is presented to an examinee, tailored representations present students with different forms of the test content. Reading aloud content, presenting text-based content in sign language or Braille, tactile representations of graphical images, symbolic representations of text-based information, narrative representations of chemical compounds (e.g., "sodium chloride" instead of "NaCl") or mathematical formulas, and translating to a different language are all forms of tailored representations.

For paper-based instructional and test materials, tailored representations often require the development of different versions or forms of the materials, or the use of translators or interpreters who present tailored representations to the student. In a digital content delivery system, tailored representations of content could be built into the content or item bank and the system should be able to tailor the representational form presented to students based on their individual needs without requiring the development of different versions of software, materials, or test forms.

Universal Design and Testing

Capitalizing on the flexibility of computer-based technologies, it is possible to personalize the presentation and representational forms of test content, interaction with that content, and response modes based on each individual's access needs. Principles of universal design play an important role in designing a system that can personalize the testing experience based on each individual student's needs.

The concept of Universal Design was spurred by the Americans with Disabilities Act of 1990 (1991), and was a direct response to design flaws in buildings – staircases, narrow entrances, escalators, high sinks, etc. – that made it difficult for people with physical disabilities to access buildings or use facilities within those buildings. In 1997, the Center for Universal Design formally defined Universal Design as "the design of products and environments to be usable by all people, to the greatest extent possible, without the need for adaptation or specialized design" (Center for Universal Design, 1997). The concept of Universal Design has extended from the field of architecture to many other arenas including product design, media, and recreation. Rather than creating a single solution, Universal Design has come to embrace the concept of allowing users to select from multiple alternatives. As Rose and Meyer (2000, p. 4) emphasize, "Universal Design does not imply 'one sizes fits all' but rather acknowledges the need for alternatives to suit many different people's needs...the essence of [Universal Design] is flexibility and the inclusion of alternatives to adapt to the myriad variations in learner needs, styles, and preferences."

In the field of education, universal design for learning (UDL) applies these same design principles by considering the variety of accessibility and learning needs of students when developing instructional materials. According to the National Center on Universal Design for Learning (2009), the three principles of UDL are as follows:

1. Provide alternative formats for presenting information (e.g., use multiple or transformable accessible media)
2. Provide alternative means for action and expression (e.g., write, draw, speak, use graphic organizers, etc.)
3. Provide alternative means for engagement (e.g., background knowledge, options, challenge, and support)

When applied to the development of curricular materials and instruction, these principles of UDL require one to consider a range of possible needs that students may have when accessing, engaging with, and responding to instructional materials and activities. Rather than building one set of materials or a single activity that is expected to work for all students, UDL encourages the development of a variety of materials and activities from which those that are most useful for a given student are selected (Rose & Lapinski, this volume).

When applied to testing, universal design has important implications for the development of test content, the interface used to deliver test items, and the interaction between the examinee, the test content, and the test interface. Technology allows developers to apply principles of universal design to educational tests such that access improves for all users. Rather than providing special accommodations, such as a separate test booklet with large print for students with reduced vision, computer-based test delivery allows magnification tools to be embedded into a delivery interface. In addition, several access tools and features can be embedded into the same testing program and activated as needed for each individual student. Finally, various methods that allow students to interact with test content and/or record responses can also be made available in a computer-based environment.

NimbleTools®: A Case Example

NimbleTools® is a universally designed test delivery system that embeds several different accessibility and accommodation tools within a single system. A few examples of accessible tools include read aloud of text-based content, oral descriptions of graphics and tables, magnification of content, altered contrast and color of content, masking of content, auditory calming, signed presentation of text-based content, and presentation of text-based content in Braille using a refreshable Braille display (i.e., a peripheral device that displays Braille characters, usually by means of raising dots through holes in a flat surface).

For students who have not been identified with one or more access needs, NimbleTools® delivers a test using a standard computer-based test delivery interface. For students who need an accommodation or set of accommodations, a test proctor/teacher settings tool is used to customize the tools available for each student. As the student performs a test, he or she is able to use available tools as needed. This flexibility allows testing programs to customize the delivery interface to meet the specific needs of each student and for the student to then use specific tools as needed for each item on the test.

To capitalize on the flexible nature in which systems such as NimbleTools® personalize the testing experience, two additional elements are required. First, test content must be developed in a manner that specifies the various representational forms in which it can be presented to students. Second, a student profile must be developed that indicates access needs and which tools and/or representational forms should be made available for each individual student.

As an example of the first element, the item displayed in Fig. 1 is part of a test designed to measure a construct labeled "eighth grade mathematics ability." One facet of eighth grade mathematics ability is the ability to calculate a median; Fig. 1 is designed to measure this facet. For a student with standard vision, solid information processing skills, and grade-level reading skills, the presentation and representational forms employed by this item do not introduce significant unintended constructs to the measure of the intended construct facet (i.e., ability to calculate a median). However, others might require adapted representations, for example:

- A magnified version of the item may be necessary for a student with lower levels of visual acuity.
- The item may need to be read aloud for a student who has difficulty in decoding text.
- A different representational form of the table may be necessary for a student who is still developing information processing skills and has difficulty in interpreting information presented in a table.
- Braille may need to be presented for a student who is blind.

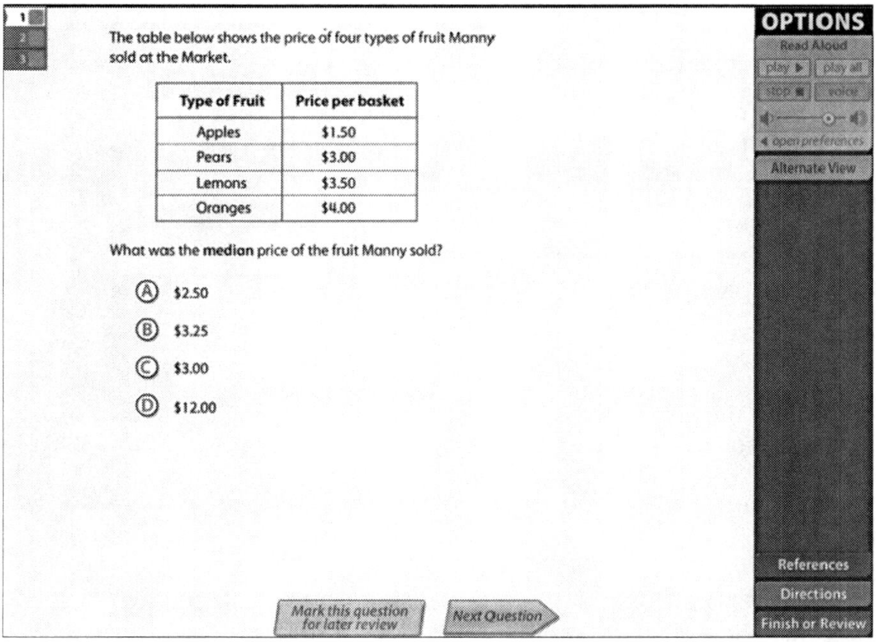

Fig. 1 Sample item designed to measure the ability to calculate a median

For some needs, such as low visual acuity, tools built into the delivery system (e.g., magnification and color tints) can be activated to help reduce the influence of the unintended construct. For other needs, such as oral and Braille presentation of text-based content and different representational forms of the content presented in the table, information must be embedded in the item itself in order to specify exactly how content is to be read aloud, presented in Braille, or presented in an alternate representation. For most content, oral and Braille versions are verbatim reproductions of the text-based content. However, some text-based content requires careful thought in how it is presented in other forms. The item depicted in Fig. 1 contains the expression "$2.50." Since the expression itself is a representation used to express a quantity of money, there are at least three ways this representation can be translated into another representational form. For example, one might read this expression as "Two dollars and fifty cents" or as "Two and a half dollars" or as "Two point five dollars," and so on. The construct being measured and the extent to which students are expected to be familiar with specific terms will influence which translation is most appropriate. That translation, then, must become part of the item content.

Similarly, Fig. 2 displays an alternate representational form of the table contained in Fig. 1. For items that do not measure a students' ability to read and interpret information presented in tabular form, an item developer might opt to include additional representational forms of specific content that allow students with different needs to access that content in different ways.

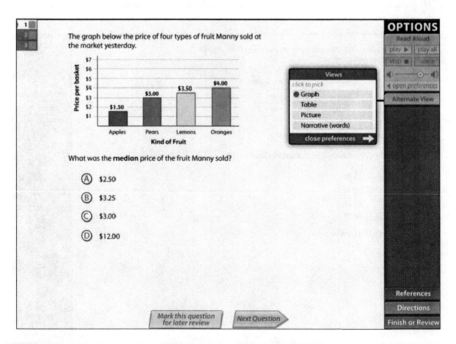

Fig. 2 Alternate representation of information presented in tabular form

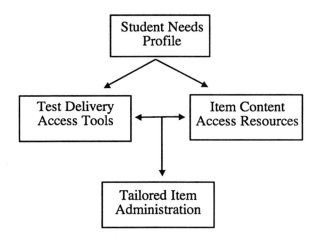

Fig. 3 Personalized test delivery model

The final element required to personalize an assessment experience is an access profile. An access profile defines access needs for a given student and indicates which tools and/or representational forms should be made available for each individual student. The profile also specifies settings, such as magnification levels, color contrasts, or default representational forms. Once defined, an access profile interacts with both the test delivery interface and the test item. The interaction with the delivery interface focuses on specific tools or features embedded in the interface, activates those tools and features that are defined in the profile, and, in some cases, controls the exact settings for those tools and features. The interaction with the test item focuses on which of the specific representational forms embedded in the item should be presented and/or activated for a given student in order to meet his or her specific need. As depicted in Fig. 3, the access profile effectively controls the behavior of the interface and the components of an item are presented to the student. The result is personalized test delivery.

Beyond Personalized Presentation of Test Items

Personalizing the presentation of test items to improve access is a powerful advancement for the field of testing. However, technology affords other ways in which tests can be personalized in order to enhance test validity. These enhancements fall into three general categories: altering content to increase engagement, guided supports to improve interactions with content, and tailoring item/task selection. These approaches are less developed than personalized presentation and have not been implemented at scale but have been used in several feasibility and pilot studies. They are doable today and represent important methods that are ripe for exploration and further research.

Altering Content

To improve student engagement and interest, test items often present a "real world" problem to students or present a context in which students are asked to apply the construct that is being measured. The most obvious example is a word problem. When measuring specific facets of mathematics, an item presents a context in which students are asked to apply a specific construct. As an example, when measuring an examinee's addition skills, a word problem may describe the number of pets a set of students in a class has and then ask the examinee to calculate the total number of pets owned by the students. For most word problems, the character's names and other objects contained in the problem are irrelevant. In fact, to create the appearance that a test is not culturally biased, item writers often capitalize on this irrelevance to use names and objects that are representative of different cultures and backgrounds. While this strategy may enhance the face validity of the test with respect to cultural bias, it likely has a differential effect on the engagement and interest level of different students. As the student population continues to grow more and more diverse, this strategy will likely become even less effective.

Similarly, the use of specific objects in word problems can differentially affect engagement depending upon a student's background and interests. As an example, August Wilson's play, *Radio Golf*, contains a scene in which a handyman describes his reaction to a seemingly simple test question:

> They handed me the test and I turned it in blank. If you had seventeen dollars and you bought a parrot for twelve dollars how many dollars would you have left? Who the hell gonna spend twelve dollars on a parrot? What you gonna do with it? Do you know how many chickens you can buy for twelve dollars? (Wilson, 2005).

While this character's reaction is extreme, it shows how irrelevant objects and names employed by a test item can affect the extent to which a student will engage with the item's content. In cases where engagement is negatively affected, the item is likely to produce an underestimate of the measured construct. When engagement is maximized, the item is likely to provide more accurate information about the measured construct.

To increase engagement, the content of test items can be personalized for each individual student. As of this writing, a dissertation study is in process that is examining the effect that personalized item content has on student engagement and performance. For this study, a set of item models that measure student's mathematics problem-solving skills are being tailored based on student's stated preferences. Each item model contains one or more names of people and objects. Prior to performing the test, each examinee is asked to list their three favorite male and female names. They are also asked to identify activities (e.g., playing soccer, playing video games, watching television, making jewelry, drawing, etc.) that they like to engage in, along with their favorite colors and things to eat. The names, objects, and activities identified by the student are used to create a version of each item that is specific to each student's preferences. While it is not yet clear how this personalization affects engagement and performance, the strategy holds promise to reduce the effect that decreased engagement has on the validity of test-based inferences.

Guided Supports

As discussed above, an examinee must fully understand and engage with the content and the associated task presented by a test item in order for that item to accurately measure the intended construct. For some students, structured support or scaffolding may be necessary to assist in identifying important content contained in an item or to fully understand the operation(s) the student is expected to do. A scaffold is a support that provides guidance to the student as he or she works on an item. Guidance may come in the form of highlighting important information in an item, breaking a multistep problem into smaller components, or providing additional information to assist the student in understanding what the problem is asking him or her to do. Interest in scaffolding test items has increased in response to federal regulations that allow some students, particularly those with cognitive disabilities, to perform modified assessments (Title I – Improving the academic achievement of the disadvantaged, 2005). For these studies, scaffolded modifications are provided after a test item has been developed for and piloted by the general population of students. However, just as information about adapted presentation and alternate representations can be built into the item itself during the item development process, scaffolding can also be specified a priori.

Depending on a student's need, scaffolding can take several forms. Perhaps the most basic level of scaffolding focuses on drawing the student's attention to important blocks of information in an item. This can be accomplished by selectively highlighting or bolding important content. Alternatively, pop-out boxes or arrows can be used to point the student to important content and supplement that content with additional instructions. As an example, knowing that some students confuse median and mean, for an item that asks a student to calculate a median, a pop-out box might point to the word median and state, "You are asked to find the median, not the mean." Similarly, for an item that displays numbers in a table, a pop-out box might point to a set of numbers and instruct, "You should work with these numbers when calculating the median."

Additional methods for providing scaffolded support include placing reading comprehension items in close proximity to the text with which the item is associated or highlighting blocks of text in a passage that are the focus of an item (e.g., measuring vocabulary knowledge using a word that appears in a passage). For some students, masks may be used to hide blocks of information and then reveal those blocks in a structured manner to help guide the student through a problem. Masks can also be combined with pop-out notes which appear as a mask is unveiled.

What is potentially powerful about embedding scaffolds into a technology-based system is that decisions about how content is scaffolded can be made while the content is being developed. Specific instructions about how to scaffold content can then be embedded in the item to ensure that a scaffold is provided in an appropriate and standardized manner. Just as importantly, this process of defining a scaffold a priori allows an item or test developer to make decisions about the extent to which a given scaffold is appropriate given the construct being measured, and thus opt not to provide that scaffold or to design the item a priori to avoid the need for the scaffold.

Tailoring Item and Task Selection

It is important to design all test items to be as accessible as possible for the widest population of students and to build in appropriate access supports to meet as many needs as possible. However, it is also important to acknowledge that in some cases access support cannot be provided for a given item or may be inappropriate due to an overlap between the intended construct and the access need. In such cases, technology-based delivery holds potential to personalize the testing experience by making informed decisions about which items or tasks are or are not appropriate for a student based on their access needs.

As an example, Fig. 4 displays an item that asks students to apply abstract reasoning skills to rotate a three-dimensional object. For a student whose engagement with tasks increases when manipulates are used, allowing the student to engage with a concrete representation of the object would interfere with the measure of the intended construct, namely abstract reasoning and visualization. Similarly, for a student with vision needs and who is accustomed to working with tactile images, this item would be very difficult to represent using a two-dimensional tactile. Thus, for both groups of students, the overlap between the construct being measured and the access needs of the students makes it difficult, if not impossible, to provide an accessible representational form that does not violate the intended construct.

In cases such as this, an item developer might indicate that the item is not accessible for students with a specific need that overlaps with the intended construct. To address this, a technology-based test delivery engine could be instructed either to seek a different item that measures the same construct yet is accessible for the student or to not present the item and not include information about this item in the student's score. While this action creates new challenges for test developers, the calculation of test scores, and reporting of results, it reduces confounding inferences about the intended construct with inaccurate measures that result from an inability to meet an access need.

This figure will be turned to a different position.

Which of these could be the figure after it is turned?

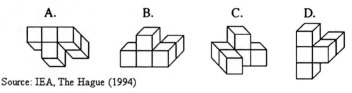

Source: IEA, The Hague (1994)

Fig. 4 Item for which tactile representation may violate construct

Bringing It All Together

For those of us who grew up bubbling in answer sheets while seated in long rows of desks in the gym, the idea of personalized assessments may feel foreign. From a test theory perspective, however, personalization has great potential to reduce error that results from needs that are irrelevant to the construct a test is designed to measure. By improving access through adapted presentation and alternate representations, some students will better understand the information with which they are asked to work. In turn, better understanding results in activation of the construct of interest. By increasing engagement with test content and the problem presented to the student, a test item has a better opportunity to capture outcomes that are the product of the construct of interest. And by allowing for multiple response modes, products of the intended construct can be recorded with greater fidelity and accuracy. Collectively, this process of personalizing assessment will result in more accurate information about the constructs of interest which in turn produces more valid inferences about student achievement.

In this age of accountability and high-stakes testing, acquiring valid measures for all students is critical. Important decisions about students, such as promotion and graduation, and about teachers and schools, such as probation and receivership, are made based on test scores. While it is difficult to know how often test scores do not provide an accurate reflection of what a student knows or can do, there is no doubt that mis-measures do occur. In fact, if we consider test accommodations, it is likely that at least 10% of the student population would be mis-measured by a test if accommodations were not allowed for students identified with a disability or special need. As we have explored in this chapter, accommodations are only one of several ways in which assessment can be personalized to provide a more accurate and valid measure for each individual student.

Today, many of the methods for personalizing assessments are achievable. In fact, while tools like NimbleTools did not exist 10 years ago, many of these methods are now being employed to varying degrees by several state testing programs. What was not possible is now becoming common practice. Other methods, like scaffolding and tailored item selection, are in early stages of development. If we are brave enough to shed the tradition of standardized conditions and make significant investments in research and development, these methods can also become commonplace in tomorrow's assessments. The promise of doing so is a more equitable, accurate, and valid assessment of achievement for all students.

References

Airasian, P. W., & Russell, M. (2008). *Classroom assessment: Concepts and applications.* New York, NY: McGraw-Hill.

Americans with Disabilities Act of 1990. (1991). Pub. L. No. 101-336, § 2, 104 Stat. 327.

Center for Universal Design. (1997). *About UD: Universal design principles.* Retrieved from http://www.design.ncsu.edu/cud/about_ud/udprincipleshtmlformat.html.

Horkay, N., Bennett, R. E., Allen, N., Kaplan, B., & Yan, F. (2006). Does it matter if I take my writing test on computer? An empirical study of mode effects in NAEP. *Journal of Technology, Learning, and Assessment, 5*(2). Retrieved from http://www.jtla.org.

Mislevy, R. J., Behrens, J. T., Bennett, R. E., Demark, S. F., Frezzo, D. C., Levy, R., et al. (2010). On the roles of external knowledge representations in assessment design. *Journal of Technology, Learning, and Assessment, 8*(2). Retrieved from http://www.jtla.org.

National Center on Universal Design for Learning. (2009). *What is UDL?* Retrieved from http://www.udlcenter.org/aboutudl/whatisudl.

Rose, D., & Meyer, A. (2000). Universal design for learning, associate editor column. *Journal of Special Education Technology, 15*(1), 66–67.

Russell, M. (1999). Testing writing on computers: A follow-up study comparing performance on computer and on paper. *Educational Policy Analysis Archives, 7*(20). Retrieved from http://epaa.asu.edu/epaa/v7n20/.

Russell, M., & Haney, W. (1997). Testing writing on computers: An experiment comparing student performance on tests conducted via computer and via paper-and-pencil. *Educational Policy Analysis Archives, 5*(3). Retrieved from http://epaa.asu.edu/epaa/v5n3.html.

Russell, M., & Plati, T. (2001). Effects of computer versus paper administration of a state-mandated writing assessment. *Teachers College Record.* Retrieved from http://www.tcrecord.org/Content.asp?ContentID=10709.

Thurlow, M. L., McGrew, K. S., Tindal, G., Thompson, S. L., Ysseldyke, J. E., & Elliott, J. L. (2000). *Assessment accommodations research: Considerations for design and analysis* (Technical Report 26). Minneapolis, MN: University of Minnesota, National Center on Educational Outcomes. Retrieved from http://education.umn.edu/NCEO/OnlinePubs/Technical26.htm.

Title I – Improving the academic achievement of the disadvantaged. (2005). Individuals with Disabilities Education Act (IDEA) – Assistance to states for the education of children with disabilities. Proposed rule. 70 Fed. Reg. 74624–74638.

Wilson, A. (2005). Radio golf. *American Theatre, 22*, 87–108.

Exploring the Minds of Innovators

Heidi Silver-Pacuilla, Tracy Gray, and Eric Morrison

Innovation

While *innovation* is the buzzword of the decade, it is hard to know what it means, particularly if you look across disciplines. From the bird's eye view of the National Center for Technology Innovation (NCTI), we wanted to explore this concept. Borrowing from the New Schools Venture Fund (Smith, 2009), we take innovation to mean "*a new approach that brings improved results...a product, platform, process, or idea...*" This definition makes clear that innovation is not merely synonymous with "new" or "creative." The "new approach" and "improved results" of the definition make it imperative that an innovation contains two key elements. First, the innovation must be put into action in a real-life setting. Second, the innovation needs to include an evaluative element to confirm the improved results. Through an ongoing series of interviews and profiles published by NCTI, we have studied innovators in educational and assistive technology for many years. This chapter explores the minds of innovators across a number of disciplines, people who have changed the game, made breakthroughs, and implemented changes that result in new approaches that make a difference.

Not surprisingly, innovation is a continuing area of study in business where the next great idea is always being pursued. Four distinct approaches to studying innovation include: categorization of innovation, whether disruptive or sustaining (Christensen, 1997; Christensen & Raynor, 2003; Christensen, Anthony, & Roth, 2004; Christensen, Horn, & Johnson, 2008); how it can be nurtured as a value and driving force (Carlson & Wilmot, 2006); how to identify productive new market spaces for it to flourish (Kim & Mauborgne, 2005); and how to harness the potential of user-centered innovation (Von Hippel, 2005). These perspectives and their implications for inclusive technology set the stage for this discussion.

Understanding whether an innovation is potentially sustaining or disruptive is critically tied to your circumstances (Christensen, 1997; Christensen et al., 2004, 2008).

H. Silver-Pacuilla (✉)
American Institutes for Research, Washington, DC, USA
e-mail: hsilver-pacuilla@air.org

T. Gray and H. Silver-Pacuilla (eds.), *Breakthrough Teaching and Learning:*
How Educational and Assistive Technologies are Driving Innovation,
DOI 10.1007/978-1-4419-7768-7_8, © Springer Science+Business Media, LLC 2011

If your business is successful and expanding, chances are high that you are not prepared to support a disruptive idea with resources and reputation. You would rather continue to expand your products and services through leaps in productivity, cost, or feature enhancements. These are *sustaining innovations* that serve your existing customer base and strengthen your brand. However, if you are a start-up entrepreneur trying to meet a new or emerging market by offering something different, cheap, or revolutionary, then *disruptive innovation* is just what you are proposing. Disruptive innovations open market space by fulfilling a new need (think Twitter) or by meeting the basic needs of current customers who feel that existing products or services have become too complex (i.e., feature-rich) to be worth the cost or user-complexity (think the simplicity of the Jitterbug phone). The educational technology landscape is fertile ground for both types of innovation. Christensen et al. (2008) consider some educational innovations disruptive; for example, online learning for very different high-school student populations (Advanced Placement and credit recovery) and flexible platforms where parents, students, and tutors can self-select learning modules to meet study needs.

Deliberately creating a culture of innovation within an organization requires five disciplines (Carlson & Wilmot, 2006): focusing on important and not just interesting needs, creating value for customers, appointing champions who lead by enthusiasm and modeling, building innovation teams, and aligning the organization. These disciplines are especially important given that:

> The exponential economy is driven by the transition to a knowledge-based economy, where one idea builds upon another at increasing speed. Knowledge compounds. Globalization hastens this process by providing more ideas. Ubiquitous, high-speed communication lets us gather those ideas faster (p. 27).

The exponential economy (note the book was written in 2006) is fast, flooded with information and ideas, and noisy (p. 137). All indicators show that the current economy is even noisier with the addition of domestic economic downturn, government involvement in key sectors, global economic turmoil, and multiple natural disasters. We learned just how interconnected and compounded our world is through the quick ramifications on the global economy of America's troubled financial system. Innovators understand that creating real value requires deliberate and direct interaction with customers as well as the marketplace of ideas which is the raw material of what is becoming possible. Focusing only on the latter inevitably results in interesting but not important developments, and the market space of assistive technologies is littered with such unusable devices that solve only imagined problems. Getting out of the laboratory to spend time in natural settings with users of assistive technology or practitioners in schools trying to implement such technologies within a structured curriculum is sure to be noisy indeed. In the final analysis, it is the only way to ensure that R&D is on track to solve important needs.

Identifying productive new market spaces for an innovation is the focus of the work of Kim and Mauborgne (2005). In a consumer-saturated culture, how can an innovator find noncustomers to appeal to? How can an innovation appeal to existing customers on entirely new dimensions? "Value innovation" is a model for "achieving a leap in value for both buyers and [businesses]" (p. 17) by balancing innovation, cost, and utility. "Unless the technology makes buyers' lives dramatically simpler, more convenient, more productive, less risky, or more fun and fashionable, it will not attract the masses" (p. 120). Kim and Mauborgne show how to find white space, or noncompetitive "*blue ocean*," where new ideas can take hold and fill a need. To identify underserved and noncustomers, industry needs to map out what it is currently being delivered to customers and where they fall short in the dimensions of utility (simplicity, convenience, productivity, risk, fun, and environmentally friendly). Kim and Mauborgne urge innovators to look across these noncustomers to look at powerful commonalities that can be amassed into a large-enough base. The potential "ease of use" population NCTI discussed in *Thriving in a Global Marketplace* (Gray, Silver Pacuilla, & Overton, 2009) call for this type of approach. What are the common access, communication, and Internet navigation needs of people with disabilities, people in rehabilitation, wounded veterans, new computer users, and the elderly? Flexibly designed solutions can serve all these populations, massing a base large enough to support new development.

Meanwhile, a parallel model looks to the general consumer for the next great idea, not as customers, but as fellow innovators. Von Hippel (2005) studies how user-centered innovation can inform the development of products and services. Looking outside manufacturing, Von Hippel sees *lead users* and *innovation communities* modifying and customizing products, platforms, processes, and ideas to meet their unique needs. The innovations created in this way are often solutions that reflect the unique setting in which they will be used, what he calls "sticky need and solution information" (p. 74). Enabling the development of such customizations happens when manufacturers make available toolkits or platforms on which savvy users can build solutions from common components and a means to share those solutions and knowledge. The willingness of users to freely reveal their innovations is well documented as a rewarding personal and social benefit. The open source movement is built on this model, with hundreds of thousands of programmers around the world contributing to Linux, Joomla, and Drupal systems; thousands of applications made available for iPhone users; and tens of thousands of books scanned and shared in Bookshare.org. This is also the world of the "long tail economy" (Anderson, 2006: see Fig. 1) in which everything, no matter how niche-specific, has a place in the marketplace of goods and services, waiting only to be found, used, and rated.

User groups can also be a source of critical input for developers. The innovators we have followed over the last 8 years have come to the AT industry from a variety of past experiences, some with no background in working with special populations whatsoever. Others have taken on development tasks due to intimate and sometimes painful personal experiences of family members, their own children, or friendships with families experiencing unmet needs. Some struggle with the daily impact of disability themselves. Still others have come from unrelated research or industry backgrounds. Their ability to recognize and understand underlying organic human factors and to intuit technical responses has struck us as uncanny in many instances. However, we have continued to be surprised at how little user

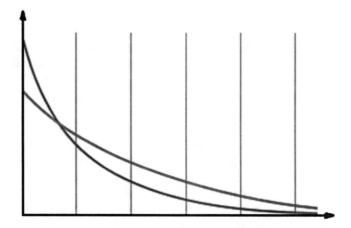

Fig. 1 The tail becomes bigger and longer in new markets (depicted with the flatter slope). In other words, whereas traditional retailers have focused on the area to the left of the chart, online bookstores derive more sales from the area to the right.

testing many developers and vendors do during development. Intuiting the needs of users with specific impairments and functional needs is hardly a substitute for pilot testing. Getting engineers and developers out of the laboratory and into real-life settings with diverse users is vital to the credibility of the tools. It is why federal agencies such as the U.S. Department of Education and the National Science Foundation make user feedback and substantive consumer involvement a requirement of research awards.

The democratization of design and development could be greatly magnified in the era of Web 2.0 knowledge bases, blogs, user communities, beta version releases, and open platforms. Several vendors of educational and assistive technologies are facilitating user groups and sharing platforms where teachers and others can share the customizations they have created for a particular curriculum unit or student need. These innovation communities are also gaining strength as sites of professional learning communities, as discussed in *The Power of Social Media for Professional Development* (Bonsignore et al., this volume).

Common Strategies

NCTI has studied innovators in education, assistive technology, and entrepreneurship over the past 8 years. Center leaders, together with author Eric Morrison, have pursued the creators of new products, platforms, processes, and ideas for what they can teach our network. Through a robust series of interviews, their compelling stories – together with the literature on innovation – illuminate some common strategies in the way innovators approach challenges that arise in the development process. Their stories also point to the imperative for our educational system to nurture innovation and creativity in our students so that they can continue to contribute to the changing future. (See the resource list at the end of the chapter for links to their online profiles and videotaped presentations.)

What is evident looking across all these innovators and models is that there are common strategies to the way innovators think and approach problems: they start by asking the right questions, they see around corners, they are not afraid to be wrong, and they can imagine new markets and opportunities.

Innovators Start by Asking the Right Questions

Christensen and his colleagues contend that customers are on the look out to "hire" a product or service to do a "job" for them. Understanding what the "job" is that consumers are trying to accomplish is the start to asking the right question. Innovators ask not just what is, but what might be? What is possible? What could happen? Two award-winning innovators, Dean Kamen and Ron Hu, exemplify how new questions spurred new thinking in the area of assistive technology development.

Dean Kamen, founder of Deka research, provided a keynote address at the 2007 NCTI conference from his stair-climbing wheelchair, the iBot Transformer. The impetus for the innovation of the iBot was not only the need for sturdy, flexible mobility, but height to level the playing field. Kamen realized the interpersonal issues that come when people look down literally and figuratively on others in wheelchairs created a social, not physical, problem. A user of the iBot gets a tool that does more than one job. It provides a new approach and improved results.

Ron Hu, an NCTI Innovator and a 2007 da Vinci award winner, saw a new opportunity lurking in two seemingly unrelated problems: unmet needs and under-used equipment at schools. Alternative and augmentative communication devices dedicated to an individual user can be very costly for families, schools, and Medicaid accounts. It often takes months if not years to fulfill a request for such a piece of assistive technology. Further, these tools are soon made obsolete as users improve, grow, and have new communication needs. Hu saw that the real "job" these devices are purchased to do is to speak for the individual who cannot speak or is not easily understood by others. A voice output engine is the core tool to hire for this job. At the same time, he saw school closets filled with hardly used portable, battery-powered word-processing devices. He developed an inexpensive voice output box that could interface with these already-available devices that would do the job at a fraction of the cost and minimal start-up training investment. This is an example of how new approaches bring about improved results for students (immediate access to a device) and schools (low cost and better utilization of equipment).

Innovators See Around the Corners

Christensen and colleagues emphasize that collected data and trends are only as good as yesterday's news and have the predictive power of a rear view mirror: "the past is a good predictor of the future only when conditions in the future resemble conditions in the past" (Christensen et al., 2004, p. xxi). In a world in which even the near future is guaranteed to be radically different than today – much less the past – we all must get much better at "seeing around the corners." Millennials expect change, as reported by the Pew Research study (2010). They are not afraid of it. Rather, the absence of rapid and revolutionizing change is unsettling to children of the future. Those of us in positions of leadership at any level need to embrace a culture of change in our work.

Michael Fullan has written extensively on leadership in education. On the culture of change, he writes,

> A culture of change consists of great rapidity and nonlinearity on the one hand and equally great potential for creative breakthroughs on the others. The paradox is that transformation would not be possible without accompanying messiness. Understanding the change process is less about innovation and more about innovativeness. It is less about strategy and more about strategizing (2001, p. 31).

Echoing Carlson and Wilmot's (2006) writing on noisy innovation communities, Fullan (2001) characterizes learning environments as (1) complex, turbulent environments [that] constantly generate messiness and reams of ideas; (2) interacting individuals [who] are the key to accessing and sorting out these ideas; and (3) "individuals [who] will not engage in sharing unless they find it motivating to do so..." (2001, p. 87). Leading "messy" and "noisy" environments while motivating smart innovative users to share their ideas is at the heart of what education should be at all levels, from pre-K through graduate school. We talk more about educational goals at the end of the chapter.

To see around corners, NCTI continues to monitor and track trends. Utilizing social media tools such as RSS feeds and social bookmarks, we compile stories, press releases, mentions, Twitter feeds, and social networks and look across the sectors of education, assistive technology, consumer electronics, and government policies to find patterns of what might be next. It is less a science than a sport, such as darts.

Innovators who have seen new applications and new markets for existing technologies exemplify the ability to see around corners. Successful initiators of tech transfers from government agencies such as NASA and the Department of Defense require the patience of Job and the persistence of Sisyphus to realize their vision. Andrew Junker, an NCTI Innovator, had such a vision that has become his second career. Junker spent a career in the U.S. Air Force studying the extreme edge of human capacity to control ultra-sophisticated electronic interfaces with brain wave control. Now, his Brainfingers technology is shattering barriers in human-technology interaction by operating as a direct interface between the user and the computer. Through a headband with embedded sensors, the system converts electrical signals across a spectrum of frequencies emanating from the brain into digitized control inputs. Users learn to control eleven channels, or virtual "fingers," to operate on-screen keyboards, communication devices, educational software, word processors, and other applications. Junker is working with users to increase usability and help them develop the necessary biofeedback mechanisms to consciously direct their own brain activity and the connected cursor on the screen. In some cases, Brainfingers has proven the only way to unlock communication from persons who have no ability to control their body or vocal cords. Early adopters include extreme gamers looking for a competitive edge, a click at the speed of thought, who found the device and were willing to try it, and an audience he did not set out to engage.

Alan Brightman, senior policy director of Special Communities for Yahoo! Inc. and former director of Apple Computer's Worldwide Disability Solutions Group, is someone who sees around corners…but not in the typical way. Reading *DisabilityLand* (2008), his award-winning book of stories, quotes, and vignettes from individuals with disabilities, one sees Alan's remarkable ability to look around the corner to capture the unofficial story. *DisabilityLand* is full of tales that could only be told after the official story had been scripted. And it is in these stories that Alan sees the promise and direction of a new way to approach existing problems and new ways to frame solutions. He is also a master storyteller, using the power of stories to motivate and enlighten. At Apple, he challenged the engineers to operate the computer and peripherals with only a pencil they could hold in their teeth. Needless to say, creative solutions were generated from this fresh perspective and challenge.

David Rose and his innovative colleagues at the Center for Applied Special Technology (CAST, http://www.cast.org) have nurtured their innovative vision not only to look around corners, but also to continue to look further upstream to solve the problem of physical and cognitive accessibility. From their start as a clinic serving individual needs, they now work on the issue at all levels, including with mainstream publishers to comply with the National Instructional Materials Accessibility Standard (NIMAS) and states in their efforts to implement accessible instructional materials (http://aim.cast.org). They have built and published tools which teachers and other instructional material producers can use that build in full accessibility and UDL principles, without having to learn any of the technical details. BookBuilder (http://bookbuilder.cast.org/) is one such tool which was launched in 2009 and already houses a library of 1,372 publicly shared, accessible e-books, complete with comprehension scaffolding. Automating accessibility of Web-published reading content through a user-friendly, social platform is an elegant solution.

Innovators Are Not Afraid to be Wrong

Malcolm Gladwell, author of *Outliers* (2008), extols the virtues of failing. Trial and error learning requires both. The very act of doing something new may lead to new directions, and all theorists of innovation emphasize the need to have time and permission to try and fail.

The reality of the "exponential economy" (Carlson & Wilmot, 2006) compels designers and creators to get their ideas out earlier and in rougher form to draw feedback and improvements from potential collaborators, critics, and users. "Knowledge compounding" is the positive way of looking at this phenomenon, but when the early drafts and prototypes are pummeled online by reviewers and competitors, it feels rather more painful. But honest user-based feedback is infinitely more important to get on a beta than on a final version when a recall might be warranted because of a mistake.

NCTI has used this approach with the publication in draft form for our annual Issue Papers on trends and directions. User feedback has resulted in an improved final product every time. When we have been unclear about our stakeholders' intentions or misread the challenges they face, we are likely to draw comments that inform and improve the final copy. In 2009, Ruth Ziolowski, president of Don Johnson, Inc., pointed out on the draft of our *Unleashing the Power of Innovation for Assistive Technology* paper that all the state-of-the-art assistive technology in the world would not help students who were not provided with technology for learning. Indeed, addressing her comments by tracking down the low numbers of students with disabilities who are taught with assistive technology led us to add a systems-level implication: "Insist that more students with disabilities have access to and are learning with AT that will promote their achievement and independence" (Gray, Silver Pacuilla, Overton, & Brann, 2010, p. 17).

Under director Larry Goldberg, the Media Access Group at WGBH Public Broadcasting in Boston maintains an extremely broad and ambitious agenda for universal media access. It is unafraid to take on particularly difficult development tasks, including bringing technologies up to speed on accessibility in very short time frames, even though complex collaborations and tight time frames introduce substantial risk not only of errors, but also of sapping resources and diluting your brand. The Media Access Group has been intimately involved with VoiceOver, the full-fledged screen reader for Apple that was developed in under a year, and Internet accessibility projects for AOL. Goldberg says,

> You can't survive without collaborating. From the get-go of any idea we immediately start asking, who can we partner with? If it's anything you want to get out to the broad population, you instantly have to think of industry – the people who bring products to the field.

Another effort built upon trial and error and knowledge compounding is Bookshare, an online library of accessible books and periodicals. Jim Fruchterman, CEO of Benetech and Bookshare.org and a 2007 MacArthur Fellow, shared at the 2007 NCTI conference the excitement and enthusiasm of making multiple, serendipitous mistakes that advanced his vision of what was possible. Bookshare relied on the power of a social network to spot and correct errors in shared scanned books since 2002, long before the interactive Web made this easy. Imperfect scanners did not stop Bookshare from building a shared library that relies on creative and passionate helpers to overcome real-world obstacles and find new ways of providing alternative text to readers with low vision, blindness, or dyslexia.

Innovators Can Imagine New Markets and Opportunities

The emerging e-culture and economy described by Anderson (2006) strongly challenge traditional manufacturing, distribution, and marketing systems. The forces of democratizing production, distribution, and connecting supply and demand through Web 2.0 tools open the economy to communities. "Pro-am" innovation communities are where professionals and amateurs collaborate, user recommendations have an equal say to marketing messages, and there is an infinite number of niche markets. A niche market is exactly what individuals with disabilities represent, with unique needs requiring customized solutions. The "problems" associated with being a niche market have been lamented among assistive technology manufacturers and vendors for years, but the emerging opportunities are there for those who see them. R. J. Cooper, an NCTI Innovator, asked when he fell into his career as a rehabilitation engineer, *When are we going to see AT products on the shelves at Radio Shack and Best Buy?* He knew that getting adaptive solutions in front of potential consumers where they already frequent would be the key to building the market.

When inventory space and mass appeal no longer matter, specialized equipment can have a place on the e-commerce shelf. Why not show a haptic glove that contains electronic wiring and devices that allow for an interface usable by blind users (see Image 6 in Exergames Get Kids Moving) alongside other peripherals for Guitar Hero at Amazon.com? Why are the adapted computer mouse shown at an AT industry trade show not returned on BestBuy.com when a user searches for an ergonomic mouse? The awareness bottleneck the AT industry has faced with access to target markets limited through key informants such as AT specialists and rehabilitation counselors can be released by direct sales to users and niche interest groups.

A positive feature of niche markets is that they are small, which means there are many, many people who are still noncustomers. The potential market is nearly limitless! However, some pockets of the AT market are well-established and mature, for example, screen readers for the vision impaired. Their market space is getting to be more "red," or competitive, than the "blue" of an early, open market. Some of the pitfalls of established markets, forewarned by business models, have already appeared. New offerings are becoming differentiated by nuanced features that appeal to the connoisseur or geek, but not the average customer, who is left with a bewildering array of choices. This situation augured the opportunity to break through with super-simple, low cost, easy to install and use, scaled down versions of screen readers, such as those appearing for free on the Internet and in Web browsers. They do not do everything, but they do enough to attract attention from current customers and interest among potential customers.

Game development is undergoing a similar shift. Having matured to Hollywood-size productions with matching budgets and timelines, the big news out of the 2010 Game Developers Conference (Kohler, 2010) was the exploding growth in small social games. These online games that can be played on social media sites such as Facebook require a fraction of the development cost, time, or resources, and result in games that are a fraction of the complexity. These developers take advantage of the reality that every demographic group is playing games online from massive multiplayer games such as World of Warcraft to poker, mah jong, and crossword puzzles. Developers of these smaller games are finding a great market in online sites, and a satisfaction in quicker production and simpler publication.

NCTI Innovator Ray Schmidt spent years helping his son with autism navigate the school system and social supports. It took years to get a communication device approved, purchased, and implemented for him. Time after time, Ray found himself helping teachers and specialists with devices that they found too complex and not intuitive. Users did not find the devices intuitive, either, and spending the time to teach sketched abstractions of simple, everyday concepts seemed like a ridiculous waste of time. Why not take pictures of the user's own grandmother, favorite fast food meal, or home and use those in the communication device? Although Ray's business was in other areas, he realized that all the functionality necessary was available in a commercial handheld and set about creating an operating system for a Hewlett Packard personal digital assistant, a system that would allow users to "build their own machines" by customizing almost every functionality. He courageously entered the AT domain, recognizing that he could leverage the power of portable technologies that had already largely become mainstream. The device, Cyrano, capitalizes on commercial functionality for a wide variety of needs from autism, communication and speech language disorder, stroke and traumatic brain injury support, workplace training supports, and so on in a device that does not begin with an assistive technology platform, but rather a common PDA.

Globalization opens up new markets, but not without new challenges. Elluminate, a Web conferencing software company based in Canada, knew well the many barriers to marketing their tools to the developing world: funding, insufficient infrastructure, unreliable electricity, inconsistent bandwidth, and wide variations in equipment capacity among conference participants. NCTI Innovator and Tech Museum Laureate Stace Wills described how all of these issues and more made for a daunting market for marketing licenses for Web conferencing. Yet recognizing a largely untapped population with endless potential growth, they created a solution on their delivery software that minimizes the impact of interruptions when they occur without downgrading the quality for those users with consistent capacity. This solution "on our end" enables Elluminate to continue to innovate and upgrade their delivery for high-bandwidth users while keeping their platform backwards compatible with the challenging realities that continue in developing markets.

What Does This Mean for Educational and Assistive Technology?

What does all of this mean for the future of assistive technology and consumers who rely upon accessible media and assistive technologies? Key trends in AT were introduced in the chapter on *Trends and Futures* (Gray et al., this volume). In 2009, NCTI stakeholders contributed to an effort to describe state-of-the-art AT and AT training. From their input, five themes emerged which include (1) convergence of tools; (2) customizability and universal design for learning; (3) portability for independence; (4) research or evidence based; and (5) interoperability (Gray et al., 2010). An overarching theme and persistent request was that applications, devices, and systems should be simple to use, implement, and maintain.

NCTI has followed these trends in technology innovation crossing over from consumer electronics to educational and assistive technology. Many products and approaches originally designed for people with disabilities are increasingly recognized as presenting solutions for the wider consumer market (Jana, 2009). Think of the hip, new touchscreen devices of all types and sizes and voice controls of everything from cell phones and car stereos to airline reservations.

The forces toward convergence, portability, and interoperability, in particular, are driving delivery of AT to the Web. Text readers are now a service to be called up as needed; translation services are a click away; and the deaf community is moving to e-mail, chat, instant messaging, text messaging, and video conferencing as the communication channels of choice over telephone relay systems.

Even augmentative communication systems are available on the Web. NCTI Innovators Faridodin "Fredi" Lajvardi and Karen Suhm at Alexicom Tech are challenging traditional notions of augmentative or alternative communication by tossing out the device and its inherent limitations and putting communication functionality on the Internet. Users and support persons quickly connect images from the Web then use existing portable computers, laptops, iPhone or iTouch devices, or a range of emerging tablet technologies to engage in icon-to-speech conversations. Pre-existing linguistic templates can be downloaded to get users set up within minutes. The system offers virtually unlimited customizability and fluid, instantaneous upgrades without the risk of a unit failing, and having to be sent off for proprietary repairs with the resulting down time.

There are obvious challenges with this trend. The first challenge is the reliance on robust and portable Internet access devices for delivery and independent use. Mobile portable formats are accessible on the go – *if* you have a Web-enabled access device. If not, users are just as dependent upon their computer and Internet connection as they would be a dedicated, unitasking device. The penetration of Web-enabled mobile devices is deep, but far from ubiquitous in the disability and low-income communities (Rainie, 2010). Even at home on desktop computers, this population is in danger of being "digitally excluded" from the broadband revolution, as cautioned by the FCC Broadband Plan (http://www.broadband.gov/). Affordability of broadband and access device service plans is a major concern for the disability community.

A second challenge is the Web delivery which allows companies to push updates to the user. When such services are updated, users might have to re-customize the program to his or her profile or re-establish interoperability with a complementary assistive technology. This growing phenomenon is confounding users of AT and custom devices. "Can we please get our heads out of the clouds?" asked Larry Goldberg at the 2009 NCTI Technology Innovators Conference. Cloud computing and Web-based delivery has much to offer, but there are many questions remaining about who has control over updating user profiles, maintaining interoperability, and accessing most useful channels.

In the world of the interactive, read–write Web, everyone can be a producer and creator of material consumed by others. We have the opportunity to learn from a new universe of producers who publish by hitting the Submit button. What is clear, however, is that production ease, speed, and volume are far outstripping understandings of accessibility or instructional design.

Users with disabilities are confronting ever-growing volumes of inaccessible content while leading providers are working to make content accessible after the fact, and government regulations guide only a minimum level of accessibility. For example, millions of videos have been posted on YouTube since it was purchased by Google in 2006, but only a fraction have been captioned for deaf and hard of hearing or audio described for the blind and visually impaired. Providing captions of TV-produced shows aired online got a boost from Oscar-winning actress Marlee Matlin who publicly complained to ABC that while she could dance on the immensely popular show "Dancing with the Stars," she could not access the online Webcasts. New solutions underway on sites such as YouTube, Hulu.com, and AOL include applying speech recognition to videos to provide basic, but imperfect, captioning.

Another emerging solution is depending on the contributions of the crowd. The reCaptcha tool, developed at Carnegie Mellon University (http://recaptcha.net/), capitalizes on common security needs for online sign-up forms to ensure humans are sending information to a Web service. These common widgets have readers discern indistinct visual images or garbled audio clips and translate them into text. By capturing all this knowledge that only humans could discern, the reCaptcha project is solving difficult problems that have arisen with the digitizing of many old or damaged documents. The project presents to the "crowd" – we, the Internet users – the images and audio clips that are not distinguishable by automated scanners and captures two or three responses for confirmation. The answers are then used to complete the transcription puzzle, making online documents more fully transcribed and accessible.

Solving the problems of accessibility through automation may be a new market for accessibility developers, but such automation will inevitably also be disruptive, challenging traditional custom AT providers unless they start competing in both markets.

What Does This Mean for Education?

What can innovators teach us about education? A great deal. Innovative thinkers are not typical students. They may not even be good students, but they are good learners. Popular culture abounds with alternative heroes who were poor performers in school but have gone on to be successful business leaders, inventors, artists, etc. We celebrate that they overcame the odds our schooling system placed in their way. Many of our NCTI Innovators have stories to tell of overcoming odds and expectations (or maybe it's odd expectations?) to achieve their creative visions.

Preparing students for a future that is radically different than today's reality means less emphasis on data showing what they knew yesterday (and if they knew it in exactly the same way the question was asked) and a lot more about preparation and tolerance for change and lifelong learning. It takes a "whole new mind" according to Pink (2005).

Pink and others (Friedman, 2005) describe a world that is facing major upheavals related to the rise of "Asia, abundance, and automation," a world where individuals and organizations must consider the following three questions:

1. Can someone overseas do it cheaper?
2. Can a computer do it faster?
3. Is what I am offering in demand in an age of abundance?

The answers to these questions can all too often be "yes." What cannot be outsourced, he argues, are the signature human aptitudes of "high concept and high touch." Pink describes six senses that can guide the development of the whole new mind, one that will be more flexible and adaptable to our globalized and challenging future: *design, story, symphony, empathy, play*, and *meaning*. These senses are what are already in the minds of innovators. They are what helps innovators design new solutions that meet understudied needs; engage teams and implementers with compelling stories; see across boundaries and disciplines to compose a symphony of synthesis; value playing with ideas; and look for connections and meaning in functional limitations, unexpected events, and objects. Looking to innovators' development can provide us with insights about *how* to nurture these talents.

One of the keen thinkers about these issues is Yong Zhao. Listening to him takes you on a globe trot of ideas, analogies, and connections. He is a one-man symphony. And yet his educational story does not start out as a prediction of such a global mindset. Born and raised in a remote, rural village in China, he has become a University Distinguished Professor at the College of Education, Michigan State University; the executive director of the Confucius Institute and the U.S.–China Center for Research on Educational Excellence; and a speaker in great demand around the world. He is called in to shake loose people's understanding of what matters in education and research and how technology can help achieve the vision. He often talks about talent, and in a manner quite different than the traditional ideas of talented athletes and musicians. He is talking about human diversity – biological, psychological, and cultural. We need all of it, he insists. *Talent diversity* complements and augments human capacity; it breeds innovation and innovators with fresh perspectives; and it prepares societies for change.

One of the innovative scholars who has challenged America's narrowing conception of intelligence is Howard Gardner of Harvard University. His theory of multiple intelligences (1983) provided a fresh perspective and robust cognitive science to free teachers' creativity in preparing instruction that appealed to different types of students in their classes. It liberated adults to understand themselves better, too, and why or why not they might have succeeded in traditional programs or workplaces where their ways of thinking were or were not valued. With *5 Minds for the Future* (2008), Gardner lays out his vision of the *habits of mind* that have characterized innovators in the past and should be cultivated to develop innovators to tackle the challenges of the future. They are habits of mind characterized as disciplined, synthesizing, creating, respectful, and ethical. Each in its way can illuminate outstanding characters from the past as well as preview success in the future.

There is obviously remarkable overlap between Dan Pink's "senses," Yong Zhao's "global mindset," and the five minds. That is a good thing. It helps us hone in on what we need to consider in making positive changes that will foster innovation.

Reinventing American schools to foster innovation and innovators is no small task. Gladwell's *Outliers* (2008) reminds us of what we often fail to see: we can change the odds by changing the policies and rules that are exclusionary rather than inclusionary. It will take acknowledging the biases that are assessed and reported by standardized tests. Zhao (2009) considers the current metrics of the American education system – performance on standardized tests and grade point averages – to be deeply flawed and eerily reminiscent of Asian countries' histories of glorifying well-defined knowledge that has resulted in an under-creative culture of "high scores and low ability." Rather than jump on the popular media bandwagon to decry the poor performance of students on international measures by reaching for ever more standardization, he exhorts us to invest in our strengths – our ability to nurture creativity, talent, and innovation. Individualism is a core American value, he reminds us, yet our educational system seems bent on a path toward standardization and narrowly defined and assessed talents. Zhao cautions us to change course and shift our focus to building an education system that cultivates skills and knowledge that are not easily outsourced; creativity; cognitive skills such as problem solving and critical thinking; and emotional intelligence. Within this broadened view, everyone's talents, knowledge, and skills are valued and can contribute to the community and society.

The National Education Technology Plan (http://www.ed.gov/technology/netp-2010) ends with a call to focus the research and social community on "grand challenge" problems that can drive innovation and knowledge building. To qualify as a grand challenge, the research problems should be:

- Understandable and significant, with a clearly stated compelling case for contributing to long-term benefits for society
- Challenging, timely, and achievable with concerted, coordinated efforts
- Clearly useful in terms of impact and scale, if solved, with long-term benefits for many people and international in scope
- Measurable and incremental, with interim milestones that produce useful benefits as they are reached (p. 77)

Addressing these research questions through "high-risk/high-gain" actions can significantly shift the odds that educational institutions and learners in them can be successfully prepared for the future. Achieving personalized learning environments for *all* students that reinforce their talents, abilities, and interests would be a real innovation. Leading the change will require innovative educators and school leaders to be champions who can help their teams adopt a new vision and enactment of education.

Champions are not lone inventors or rock star teachers. Innovation, as stated at the beginning of the chapter, requires that the new approach be put into action in a real-life setting and evaluated to check results. There will be a lot of trial and error learning, some ideas will be found to be wrong, and some team members will be unable to cross the gap to the new vision. Champions have to be passionate and articulate leaders who are committed to the vision, not the system with its current performance metrics or team members.

The job description of an innovation champion is laid out in Carlson and Wilmot (2006): "[Y]our job is to align all the elements of your team, keep them focused, and constantly work in the direction of change while valuing what you already have" (p. 225). The real challenge is getting the team aligned:

> Most of us get paralyzed in the face of change. The movement to something new requires crossing a deep void – a subconscious barrier. We perceive a gap between the old vision and the new vision, a bottomless pit into which we might fall. It appears because we are not sure that we will be successful and valued in the new vision or assignment…The secret of crossing the void is deceptively simple. The secret: We must see a way to *leverage our current strengths in the new innovation's vision.* Some of us will be able to make this transformation on our own, but most of us need help from our significant others, colleagues and other champions. As champion…helping all the members of your team to cross the void is your responsibility and one of your first priorities (p. 228).

Helping others see, feel, and accept change to set out on a new path is not for the faint of heart. In fact, Heath and Heath (2010) advise relying on the services of a rider and an elephant. Drawing on Haidt (2006), they describe how individuals and teams behave simultaneously as rational analysts (riders) and as an emotional energy force (elephant). Using a wealth of examples and stories, they describe the strengths and weaknesses of each and how to motivate change. Getting the rider and elephant in each of us and on teams to work together, their research suggests, requires directing the rider without letting him or her get bogged down in analysis and motivating the elephant by finding the feeling and shrinking the (perceived) scope of the change.

Conclusion

Meeting the challenges of today and tomorrow – both the human and the technological – will require innovation that brings improved results. From challenges of an aging population to an unprecedented oil spill a mile under the Gulf of Mexico, the potential is obvious for advanced technologies to contribute to creative solutions. An exploration of the process of innovation and the minds of innovators reveals key characteristics and decision points that can be leveraged to make innovation more likely and more efficient. From a funding and sponsorship perspective, successful innovation requires team work, time for trial and error, and consumer input. For educators, nurturing innovative thinking means building upon students' strengths and talents beyond their demonstrated performance on tests and teaching to the new habits of mind described by Pink (2005) and Gardner (2008). We need to foster the innovative spirit in each of us to embrace and seek change that will open new opportunities for others.

Appendix

Visit the innovators		
Alan Brightman	Senior Policy Director, Special Communities, Yahoo! Inc.	http://www.nationaltechcenter.org/videos/exploring-DisabilityLand/
R. J. Cooper	Founder, RJ Cooper and Associates	http://www.nationaltechcenter.org/innovators/beyond-switches/
Jim Fruchterman	Founder and CEO, Benetech and Bookshare.org	http://www.nationaltechcenter.org/videos/fruchterman-keynote/
Larry Goldberg	Director, Media Access, WGBH	http://www.nationaltechcenter.org/innovators/media-access-group/; http://www.nationaltechcenter.org/videos/national-accessible-technology-plan/
Ron Hu	President and Designer, Afforda Speech	http://www.nationaltechcenter.org/innovators/augmentative-communication/
Andrew Junker	Founder, Brain Actuated Technologies (BAT)	http://www.nationaltechcenter.org/innovators/brain-actuated-technologies/
Ray Schmidt	Vice President, OneWrite Company	http://www.nationaltechcenter.org/innovators/oneWrite-cyrano-communicator/
Stace Wills	Global Director, Fire and Ice (Elluminate)	http://www.nationaltechcenter.org/innovators/applying-social-entrepreneurship/
Faridodin "Fredi" Lajvardi and Karen Suhm	Co-Founder and Web Systems Developer, Alexicom Tech	http://www.nationaltechcenter.org/innovators/alexicom-tech/

References

Anderson, C. (2006). *The long tail: Why the future of business is selling less of more*. New York: Hyperion.

Brightman, A. (2008). *DisabilityLand*. New York: Select Books.

Carlson, C. R., & Wilmot, W. W. (2006). *Innovation: The five disciplines for creating what customers want*. New York: Crown Business.

Christensen, C. M. (1997). *The innovator's dilemma*. Boston, MA: Harvard Business School Press.

Christensen, C. M., Anthony, S. D., & Roth, E. A. (2004). *Seeing what's next: Using the theories of innovation to predict industry change*. Boston, MA: Harvard Business School Press.

Christensen, C. M., Horn, M. B., & Johnson, C. W. (2008). *Disrupting class: How disruptive innovation will change the way the world learns*. New York: McGraw Hill.

Christensen, C. M., & Raynor, M. E. (2003). *The innovator's solution: Creating and sustaining successful growth*. Boston, MA: Harvard Business School.

Friedman, T. H. (2005). *The world is flat*. New York: Farrar, Straus and Giroux.

Fullan, M. (2001). *Leading in a culture of change*. San Francisco: Jossey-Bass.

Gardner, H. (1983). *Frames of mind: The theory of multiple intelligences.* New York: Basic Books.

Gardner, H. (2008). *5 Minds for the future.* Boston, MA: Harvard Business Press.

Gladwell, M. (2008). *Outliers: The story of success.* New York: Little, Brown and Company.

Gray, T., Silver Pacuilla, H., & Overton, C. (2009, January). *Learning and assistive technology: Thriving in a global marketplace.* Washington, DC: American Institutes for Research. http://www.nationaltechcenter.org/Uploads/2009/01/learning_assistive_technology.pdf.

Gray, T., Silver Pacuilla, H., Overton, C., & Brann, A. (2010, January). *Unleashing the power of innovation for assistive technology.* Washington, DC: American Institutes for Research. http://www.nationaltechcenter.org/documents/unleashing_the_power_color.pdf.

Haidt, J. (2006). *The happiness hypothesis: Finding modern truth in ancient wisdom.* New York: Basic Books.

Heath, C., & Heath, D. (2010). *Switch: How to change things when change is hard.* New York: Broadway Books.

Jana, R. (2009, September 24). How tech for the disabled is going mainstream. *Business Week.* Retrieved February 19, 2010, from http://www.businessweek.com/magazine/content/09_40/b4149058306662.htm.

Kim, W. C., & Mauborgne, R. (2005). *Blue ocean strategy: How to create uncontested market space and make the competition irrelevant.* Cambridge, MA: Harvard Business School Press.

Kohler, C. (2010, March 10). GDC: Big designers find satisfaction in small games. *Wired.* Retrieved from http://www.wired.com/gamelife/2010/03/gdc-small-games.

Pew Research Center. (2010). *Millennials: Confident. Connected. Open to change.* http://pewsocialtrends.org/assets/pdf/millennials-confident-connected-open-to-change.pdf.

Pink, D. H. (2005). *A whole new mind: Moving from the information age to the conceptual age.* New York: Penguin.

Rainie, L. (2010). *Internet, broadband, and cell phone statistics.* Pew Internet and the American Life Project. http://www.pewinternet.org/Static-Pages/Trend-Data/Whos-Online.aspx.

Smith, K. (2009). *Innovation in public education: Problems and opportunities.* San Francisco: NewSchools Venture Fund. Retrieved October 19, 2009, from http://www.newschools.org/files/innovation-in-education.pdf.

Von Hippel, E. (2005). *Democratizing innovation.* Cambridge, MA: MIT Press.

Zhao, Y. (2009). *Catching up or leading the way: American education in the age of globalization.* Alexandria, VA: ASCD.

Index

T. Gray and H. Silver-Pacuilla (eds.), *Breakthrough Teaching and Learning:*   145
How Educational and Assistive Technologies are Driving Innovation,
DOI 10.1007/978-1-4419-7768-7, © Springer Science+Business Media, LLC 2011

CPSIA information can be obtained at www.ICGtesting.com

227300LV00005B/6/P